Nietzsche
A Beginner's Guide

ONEWORLD BEGINNER'S GUIDES combine an original, inventive, and engaging approach with expert analysis on subjects ranging from art and history to religion and politics, and everything in between. Innovative and affordable, books in the series are perfect for anyone curious about the way the world works and the big ideas of our time.

anarchism
aquinas
artificial intelligence
the beat generation
biodiversity
bioterror & biowarfare
the brain
the buddha
censorship
christianity
civil liberties
classical music
climate change
cloning
conservation
cold war
crimes against humanity
criminal psychology
critical thinking
daoism
democracy
dyslexia
energy
engineering
the enlightenment
epistemology
evolution
evolutionary psychology
existentialism
fair trade
feminism

forensic science
french revolution
history of science
humanism
islamic philosophy
journalism
lacan
life in the universe
literary theory
machiavelli
mafia & organized crime
magic
marx
medieval philosophy
middle east
NATO
the northern ireland conflict
oil
opera
the palestine–israeli conflict
philosophy of mind
philosophy of religion
philosophy of science
postmodernism
psychology
quantum physics
the qur'an
racism
renaissance art
the small arms trade
sufism

Nietzsche
A Beginner's Guide

Robert Wicks

ONEWORLD
OXFORD

A Oneworld Book

First Published by Oneworld Publications as
Nietzsche (Oneworld Philosophers), 2002
First published in the *Beginner's Guide* series 2010

ISBN 978–1–85168–757–2

Cover design by vaguelymemorable.com
Printed and bound in Great Britain by CPI Cox & Wyman

Oneworld Publications
UK: 185 Banbury Road, Oxford, OX2 7AR, England
USA: 38 Greene Street, 4th Floor, New York, NY 10013, USA

The ideal of the most exuberant, life-filled, world-affirming person, who has not only learned to make peace with and to tolerate, what was and is, but who wants further to have just *how it was and is* repeated throughout all eternity, insatiably calling out "*da capo*," not only to himself, but to the entire performance and show.

Beyond Good and Evil, §56

Cynicism is the unique form in which unpolished souls can come into contact with what honesty is. And the higher ones should open their ears to every coarse and refined piece of cynicism, and consider it fortunate, when the joker without shame or the scientific satyr speaks out to them.

Beyond Good and Evil, §26

I do not want to be a saint; better to be a jester. Perhaps I am a jester.
Ecce Homo, "Why I am an Inevitability," §1

I am a disciple of the philosopher Dionysus; I'd prefer to be a satyr, rather than a saint.

Ecce Homo, Preface

For Catherine, Florence, Elaine and Charles

Contents

Preface

Some problems are universal. Alexandra David-Néel (1868–1969) – the first European woman to explore the Tibetan capital of Lhasa (in 1924, in disguise) – was once given the same pragmatic advice by an unnamed hermit in the remote Himalayan wilderness as was offered to Nietzsche's fictional character, Zarathustra, when he expressed his own desire to communicate his mountaintop-inspired thoughts to the general population. The hermit counselled David-Néel to resist publishing her knowledge of the "secret oral teachings in Tibetan Buddhist sects," because it probably would be a wasted effort. The teachings could be published surely enough, but they would remain "secret" nonetheless, for few ears would be in tune with their message. Like Nietzsche's *Thus Spoke Zarathustra – A Book for All and None* (1883–85), David-Néel would be writing from the spiritual heights an essentially closed book, and would be offering an invitation to be misunderstood, neglected, and possibly condemned.

Having decided to brush against the social fiber, both David-Néel – religious scholar, adventurer, person-of-wisdom, and a prime candidate for a Nietzschean superhuman in her own right – and Zarathustra made light of the soberly hermetic advice and proceeded to put their thoughts into writing. Nietzsche's philosophy, in particular, ended up expressing the frustration of the perennial tension between sociality and individuality, along with the uneasy interdependency between respectable tradition and the irreverent avant-garde. Nietzsche's external life might have been unassuming, but he often experienced at a spiritual level the solitude of the absolute monarch whose distanced position requires the sacrifice of equal-to-equal friendships and comfortable community.

And thus was his *Zarathustra* written "6000 feet beyond people and time," from a perspective that few, if any, of us will ever be able to appreciate abundantly from the inside. Perhaps Friedrich Nietzsche will never be understood as he wished to be understood, for how difficult it is to "overcome," or go perspectivally above, almost every ideal type that human culture has set forth to date as a matter of spiritual nourishment and cultural integration – above the ascetic priest, above the great-souled, magnanimous person of classical virtue, above the recognitions bestowed by worldly fame, above the greatest actors, actresses, and musicians, and above most of what we imagine to be the worthy dedications of our lives.

Perhaps Nietzsche was somewhat mistaken about his having been able to discern future social tendencies and, very possibly, over-zealous in his dedication to set forth the optimal conditions for a reinvigorating, down-to-earth health and flourishing. Such shortcomings would, fortunately, have the effect of rendering his thought more accessible than a more perfect realization of it might have allowed. And yet, despite its limitations, Nietzsche offers us some trying challenges, most of which amount to a dare to define ourselves realistically as complicated, living, now-existing, perishable, and thoroughly embodied creative creatures, as opposed to being a set of purely rational, eternal, and essentially simple souls, which are thought to be spatially, temporally, and only temporarily incarcerated in an alien physicality. Nietzsche longed for release and redemption within this world, not another one; he longed for what he took to be real, rather than imaginary, freedom.

Some of the themes treated in this survey of Nietzsche's outlook – his doctrines of eternal recurrence, the will to power, the superhuman, the death of God, perspectivism, his critique of Christian morality, his intellectual relationships to Immanuel Kant and Arthur Schopenhauer, his friendship with Richard Wagner, his influence on contemporary European thought – have been individually treated by numerous Nietzsche scholars in longer, more detailed works. The bibliography will, I hope, direct those whose interest in Nietzsche has been stimulated by this study to enhance and transform their appreciation of his radical ideas. Of special note is the impeccable work of Maudemarie Clark, whose attention to Nietzsche's theory of knowledge has influentially structured the perspective offered here. I am also indebted to an anonymous reviewer of the manuscript and to my colleague at the University of Auckland, John Bishop, both of whom provided perceptive and constructively detailed criticisms of each chapter. My own approach to Nietzsche tends to reflect an interest in the existential and psychological import of philosophical theories.

Nietzsche's multi-layered texts present a formidable task for anyone who intends to outline their general contours. It is hoped that despite the very wide differences in interpretation among scholars, the present work succeeds in portraying the importance of change, expansion, self-criticism, and life-energies within his philosophy. It can be said that Friedrich Nietzsche was the jester of metamorphosis, and that final interpretations of his thought run contrary to the unpredictable, tempting, and sometimes contemptible spirit of the mythic trickster. So this book is best regarded as one entrance into the fiery carnival of Nietzsche's thought, rather than as an ending, conclusion, or cap.

I extend further thanks to those teachers, scholars, friends, and students, living and deceased, who have motivated and encouraged my reflections on Nietzsche's philosophy from an assortment of life's angles: William H. Hay †, Herbert Garelick, Kathleen Higgins, Jack Kline, Graham Parkes, Roger Peters, Jason

Pilkington, Martin Schwab, Ivan Soll, Robert C. Solomon, Stephen Solnick, Paul Warren, Craig Wattam, Kenneth Westphal, Terry Winant, Julian Young, and Mitchell and Jill Zingman.

I also thank especially those Helens of Troy whose awakening presence in my life helped me appreciate Nietzsche's immaculate conception of Apollonian women: Gladys Eugenia Bustos-Giraldo, Susan Beth Silverberg, and Lisa Michelle Thompson.

The translations from the original German texts are my own.

Auckland, New Zealand
September 2001

The churchyard echoes of Röcken

From Jerusalem to Athens

If, as a Friedrich Nietzsche aficionado, one makes the "honored birthplace" pilgrimage to the German town of Röcken, one will be struck by the unassuming plainness of the roadside village. Röcken, located in the pastoral farmlands south of Leipzig, is a town too small for most maps: the village's more expanded name is Röcken bei Lützen (Röcken near Lützen), and one will inevitably make one's way first to Lützen. After passing through this moderate-sized community, a small cluster of buildings will soon appear alongside the main road, and if one's eyes are keen, one will pick out a church building nestling among them. It was in this churchyard that Friedrich Nietzsche played as a boy, and it was in the large house next to the church – the one designated for the pastor and his family – where Nietzsche was born on 15 October 1844. Today, over a century and a half later, it is maintained as a historical site.

Nietzsche's childhood was steeped in Lutheranism. His great-grandfather was a Lutheran minister, as were both of his grandfathers, as was his father. Little Nietzsche imagined that he would become a minister as well. One can imagine the youngster peeking through the doorway as his father gave his Sunday sermons, and maybe, as any child in such circumstances might, playing around the pulpit during the quiet countryside afternoons. The intimacy of the humble church and its surroundings is distinctive, and during the off-hours, the child could only have made himself familiar with every inch of the church's interior, which was situated literally in his family's backyard. In a real sense, Friedrich Nietzsche began his life in church.

Although Nietzsche's childhood appears to have been predominantly happy, it was also unforgettably stamped with death. When Nietzsche was approaching his fifth birthday, his father died from a brain ailment, and within only six months, the life of Nietzsche's younger brother, Joseph, who was only two years old, was ended by sickness as well. This was a terrible time for Nietzsche, as his own reported nightmares confirm.[1] Throughout his life, death's shadow followed Nietzsche in the images of his father and little brother.

With the death of Röcken's pastor, the Nietzsche family moved to the nearby city of Naumburg, where Friedrich lived with his mother, his sister, his two aunts, and his grandmother, until he entered the prestigious Schulpforta boarding school at the age of fourteen. It is fair to say that Nietzsche's dramatic loss of significant male figures within his household at an early age, side-by-side with an overdetermination of living female figures, had a formative and lasting influence on his psyche.

The academic atmosphere at Schulpforta was disciplined and cloisterlike, and in a broad sense, Nietzsche's environment did not radically change: Schulpforta opened his imagination to the Greek and Latin classics, but he remained in the Christian rural world and continued to be nurtured on Lutheran values – ones which soon became amalgamated with affectionate feelings for his German homeland. During these teenage years, Nietzsche and a few of his friends formed a tiny club which they named "Germania," the activities of which included a fateful subscription to a contemporary music periodical.

Through the club's subscription to the music journal, the *Zeitschrift für Musik*, Nietzsche became familiar with the compositions of Richard Wagner (1813–83) – a composer whose works embodied many of the religious and cultural themes that captured the young Nietzsche's heart, and for whom Nietzsche would develop a tremendous admiration in the years to come. Although he would never compare to Wagner as a composer, Nietzsche was not without considerable musical sensitivity, and by the time he reached his late teens he was writing music that could be played or sung respectably in church. Many of his compositions were stylistically reminiscent of those by Robert Schumann (1810–56), and can easily be mistaken for them by the naïve ear. At this time in his life, Lutheranism, choral and piano music, academic studies, and Germany, all coalesced within Nietzsche's mind.

To understand the transformations that occurred in Nietzsche's life once he entered college, we can reflect for a moment on some of the Christian ideas with which he grew up. One of the first that was impressed upon him – one not unique to Christianity, and which is at least as ancient as the Egyptians and their pyramidic tombs – was the concept of a world "beyond" the earthly one we inhabit, conceived of as a place to which people's souls travel after their mundane death. Immediately after his father's funeral, Nietzsche received a benevolent letter from a Lutheran pastor assuring him that his father, now standing before the throne of the Heavenly Father, continued to look down upon him from the higher world, wishing him well. At a very early age, he was impressed with the concepts of God, death, and the afterlife.

Another religious idea that entered Nietzsche's highly reflective mind, and which appears significantly in his later writings, is the persistent question of why a Heavenly Father would allow not only his own father to be taken from him, but also his innocent two-year-old brother. Christians have struggled to find an adequate solution to this "problem of evil," and witnessing the death of his younger brother only made the problem more dramatic for Nietzsche. From an early age, he was exposed to questions surrounding the meaning of life, of death, and of the world itself, all set within the atmosphere of accepting the existence of a morally good, all-seeing being called the "Heavenly Father" who was defined by his own fatherly elders as the object of unconditional love. In sum, Friedrich Nietzsche grew up as a Christian, and his personal life was marked by tragic events which eventually led him to question the Christian outlook and valuation of life, including the idea that the cosmos is, at its core, morally and good-naturedly constituted.

In 1864, when he entered the University of Bonn as a theology and philology student at the age of nineteen, life changed for Nietzsche. Not only was he situated relatively far from home for the first time, his university studies in philology also took a deep hold upon him. These drew his scholarly interests further away from the study of biblical texts towards that of the Greek and Latin classics – a field into which he been initiated at Schulpforta. Nietzsche was reborn in Bonn, for he loosened the bonds of the church-related world he inherited from his father and his rural upbringing, and soon developed what turned out to be a lifelong affection for Athens and Rome, always set in an uneasy and ambivalent contrast to Hebraic and Arabic Jerusalem. It is well-known that Nietzsche ranted against Christianity at the end of his career, but his attitude towards Middle Eastern culture in general was less cut and dried: while scorning institutionalized Christianity and its roots in Judaism, Nietzsche discerned important virtues in both the Hebrew Scriptures and in Christian asceticism, and he later chose as the figurehead for his own philosophic vision the character of Zarathustra, the Persian prophet of Zoroastrianism. The prophetic Nietzsche derived much of his historical inspiration from the Middle East, despite his condemnation of the highly institutionalized European Christianity that later prevailed closer to his home in Germany.

Despite the various doctrinal changes that were to characterize his philosophical thought, Nietzsche's love of music remained rock-solid, and in Bonn he developed his artistic interests, along with his attraction to the classics. Nietzsche studied with a biographer of Mozart, Otto Jahn (1813–69), who was the same age Nietzsche's father would have been, and who had been academically trained by Karl Lachmann (1793–1851), a well-known philologist of the time. Lachmann specialized in the Roman philosopher Lucretius (98–55 BC), and in the study of "textual recension" – a genealogical dimension of philology which determines the original authorship of texts by comparing and contrasting secondary and derivative versions. This idea of "genealogy" would later become central to Nietzsche's own philosophical style. Nietzsche was also taught by Friedrich Ritschl (1806–76), a specialist in the Roman classics, who was particularly expert on the Roman comic poet Plautus (254–184 BC).[2] All of these subjects – classics of tragedy and comedy, genealogy, music, philology – remained with Nietzsche for the rest of his scholarly life.

During his university studies in the mid-1860s, Nietzsche made the momentous encounter, either through the legacy of their books or in person, of two of the most influential figures of his life – the recently deceased Arthur Schopenhauer (1788–1860) and the still living Richard Wagner (1813–83). Both men became his heroes, but sharing the fate of many heroes and idealized father-figures, they were to be replaced by others whom he grew to idealize, ultimately being unseated by the notion of a larger-than-life, super-healthy type of Nietzsche's own creation. In the end, as we shall see, having become disillusioned with existing examples, Nietzsche became his own teacher, and styled for himself his own ideal in the form of the superhuman, or *Übermensch* – a super-healthy, super-strong, and yet far from supernatural type. As the years went on, he tended to measure famous individuals against this idealization, offering his applause for Caesar, Napoleon, Goethe, Dostoevski, Thucydides, and the Sophists, while at the same time roasting characters such as

Rousseau, Hugo, Sand, Michelet, Zola, Renan, Carlyle, Mill, Eliot, Darwin, and Dante.

In 1865, when still at the outset of his intellectual odyssey, the twenty-one-year-old Nietzsche came across Arthur Schopenhauer's *The World as Will and Representation*, which had originally been published forty-seven years earlier, in 1818. Schopenhauer achieved fame only at the end of his life, however, and his name was a new and fashionable one within academically-legitimated circles when Nietzsche discovered him for himself. Schopenhauer's philosophy revealed to the still-impressionable Nietzsche a way to interpret the world that, despite having an atheistic twist, shared much of the Christian sentiment with which Nietzsche grew up, as well as the classical Greek philosophy with which he had become enamored. While retaining in substance the traditional Christian moral imperative to resist harming others, Schopenhauer advanced a metaphysical vision that was at odds with Christianity: in the place of an all-powerful, all-knowing, and all-good God at the ruling center of the universe, Schopenhauer substituted a blind, aimless, and fundamentally senseless energetic urge that he could describe as nothing more than the blind force of sheer "will."

Schopenhauer did not explain this "will" in reference to physical forces. He turned the usual conception inside-out, and explained physical forces in reference to the manifestation of an essentially non-physical "will," which he defined as the "inner" force that metaphysically underlies all things in the cosmos, just as one's conscious will is the inner force that motivates and animates one's observable bodily actions. Schopenhauer believed that if we direct our attention to the mental energy that we use, for example, to move our hand when we will it to move, then we can have an intuitive feel for the kind of energy that moves the universe, or, more precisely, obtain a bare sense of the energy which itself constitutes the universe. The energies of the universe flow through everything, so they flow through us. And according to Schopenhauer, our will is nothing more than a refined manifestation of this blind cosmic will.

Schopenhauer accounted for the evil in the world partly in terms of the nature of this universal will itself, which he described as a pure, aimless, raw striving. Contributing to this account, and completing the picture, is the constitution of our minds. For, given the kind of analyzing and systematizing minds we happen to have, we are obliged to perceive this universal will as an energy that manifests itself objectively as a world extended in space and time, and as filled with individual things. For Schopenhauer, the individual things in the world – among which are numbered our physical bodies – are images we have constructed for ourselves. He believed that our experiences of a world that contains inherently selfish, self-serving, competing, and violent beings, whether we realize it or not, is a grand construction of our own intellectual making.

Salvation – conceived of as akin to a spiritual salve for the world's frustrating and self-conflicting nature – Schopenhauer discovered through artistic (especially musical), moral, and ascetic-religious-mystical experience. He argued that by listening to music, or by contemplating a painting or sculpture, we can temporarily lift ourselves out of our daily worries and our mundane way of intellectualizing and individualizing the world. He conceived of aesthetic experience as a balm for dissatisfaction, as a gaze at universality, and as a transcendence of the finite human condition.

Schopenhauer's view appealed to Nietzsche, for it allowed him to hold on to his inherited Christian morality, while it also liberated him from an all-seeing watcher – not to mention a moral judge and executioner – in the heavenly skies. At this point, Nietzsche was less troubled by the effects of traditional moral values themselves, than by the super policing-force that allegedly enforces these values, namely, a powerful guilt-generating being called "God" who absolutely penetrates everyone's mind and spiritual privacy. Schopenhauer's philosophy had the merit of recognizing no intrusive God, even though it preserved Christian moral values. Schopenhauer also allowed Nietzsche to contemplate more clearly what must have been prodding at the back of his mind for years – the suspicion that in itself, the world might lack intrinsic meaning and redeeming value. This painful, and yet also potentially liberating, thought rose to the surface in Nietzsche's reading of Schopenhauer, and it led him to confront – in a forceful, explicit, and intellectually sophisticated manner – the possibility that God might not exist.

Schopenhauer also supported Nietzsche's enthusiasm towards an assortment of non-monotheistic interpretations of the world – ones that included not only Schopenhauer's particular brand of atheism, but also the more polytheistic and mythic worlds of ancient Greece with which he had been familiar. For at least the next seven years of Nietzsche's development, the Greek mythical outlook stood side-by-side with Schopenhauer's atheistic one, and Nietzsche's philosophical reflections can be conveniently described during this period as fundamentally Schopenhauerian, and as displaying an increasing predominance of ancient Greek influence as time progressed. Soon, during the late 1870s, this amalgam was transformed by Nietzsche's growing interest in the scientific, biological, and physiological perspectives that were gaining currency during the second half of the nineteenth century. The creative, imaginative, visionary, myth-loving artist and the cool, objective, reality-seeking scientist formed an unstable mix, as they combined and recombined continually within Nietzsche's struggling and aspiring mind. The tension was paralleled by his efforts to interpret the world as a meaningful place which could ground a desire to live, side-by-side with a deep suspicion that, objectively considered, the world is intrinsically meaningless and life is without a point.

Nietzsche's other hero during his early twenties was Richard Wagner. He had known of Wagner's music as a teenager, and as he was about to complete his studies in classical philology at the University of Leipzig – the institution to which he had followed his teacher, Ritschl, in 1865 – he was personally introduced to Wagner. Partly on the basis of their shared enthusiasm for Schopenhauer, the two men struck up a father–son style of friendship (Wagner, like Otto Jahn, was born in the same year as Nietzsche's father), and they remained in contact for the next decade, until Nietzsche's growing anti-Christian view of life became incompatible with Wagner's more traditionally Christian, albeit German-mythic, outlook.[3] Wagner's anti-Semitism also began to upset Nietzsche, and Nietzsche's enthusiasm for Schopenhauer also waned.[4] Wagner also had become a cultural superstar by this time, while Nietzsche had remained an unknown.

Wagner loomed large in Nietzsche's reflections to the very end, and until immediately prior to his collapse in January 1889, Nietzsche continued to define himself against Wagner, fighting inwardly to avoid being eclipsed by his conception of the man. Their eventual differences notwithstanding, Nietzsche found in Wagner an intellectual equal, a musical superior worthy of respect, the embodiment of a social ideal (given Wagner's fame), a substitute father-figure, and a person who helped channel his literary energies in a productive, if not competitive, manner.

One notable result was Nietzsche's first book, *The Birth of Tragedy, Out of the Spirit of Music*, which integrated the themes that had been circulating within Nietzsche's life – the meaning and value of existence, the Greeks, music, tragedy – and which concluded by celebrating Wagner's music, alongside that of Bach and Beethoven, as the potential savior for Germany's, and Europe's, weakening cultural spirit. The book was rich in thematic material, and it stood as a tribute to his older friend. But Nietzsche paid a high price for his celebration of Wagner's music and for his critique of contemporary German culture: the book's grandiose aspirations, along with its imaginative style and scope, did little to enhance Nietzsche's academic reputation as a classical philologist.

During their best times together, Nietzsche and Wagner shared a common intellectual ground in the philosophy of Arthur Schopenhauer – a philosophy written with artists, ascetics, and mystics positively in mind. Schopenhauer's views were somewhat ahead of their time for the nineteenth-century philosophical world, and it was uncommon for anyone to claim that even though the world was godless, salvation was possible through the arts, and especially through music, supposedly the highest art. Schopenhauer's core assertion that the world is fundamentally absurd was a bold proposition for 1818, for such views did not become common currency until the next century, in the aftermath of the First World War. For Nietzsche and Wagner to read, moreover, that music was the highest, the most profound, and the art form most akin to the ultimate truth, must have been music to their ears.

Perhaps more significantly in relation to Nietzsche's philosophical concerns, though, Schopenhauer believed that salvation from the world's ills could be achieved by cultivating a level of expanded consciousness through which one's finite individuality could be oceanically dissolved – a level within which one could identify oneself more broadly with the entire cosmos or, alternatively, feel oneself in unity with the heartbeat of humanity. This, for Schopenhauer, was the level of moral consciousness, where the pains and joys of other people become none other than one's own pains and joys, and where the act of hurting another being becomes none other than the act of hurting oneself. This standpoint has noticeably Christian overtones, and prior to Schopenhauer, it was expressed memorably by the poet, John Donne (1572–1631) in 1624:

Who bends not his ear to any bell which upon any occasion rings?
But who can remove it from that bell which is passing a piece of
himself out of this world? No man is an island entire of itself; every
man is a piece of the continent, a part of the main. If a clod be
washed away by the sea, Europe is the less, as well as if a promon-
tory were, as well as if a manor of thy friend's or of thine own
were. Any man's death diminishes me, because I am involved in
mankind. And therefore never send to know for whom the bell
tolls: it tolls for thee.[5]

Arthur Schopenhauer and the problem of evil

The problem of evil, as formulated within the Western philosophical and theological traditions, presupposes that one acknowledges
a majesterial God who is all-knowing, all-powerful, and all-good.
If such a being exists, then the existence of evil becomes a moral
mystery. On the face of things, an all-good God would desire to
eliminate evil; an all-knowing God would know how to eliminate evil; an all-powerful God would be able to eliminate evil.
Evil should not exist, if God exists, because everything should
already be perfect, precisely because the world is the product of a
perfect creator. It is painfully apparent, however, that the world is
filled with suffering. So either God does not exist, or God has
reasons to allow evil to exist, although such reasons might be
inscrutable to human beings. Owing to evil's existence, one must
therefore either abandon the belief in God's perfectly allied
omnibenevolence, omniscience, and omnipotence, or, accepting
that such a God exists, discern the divine reasons for evil's existence, or, if failing in that superhuman effort, engage in humanly
reasonable speculation about God's difficult-to-grasp ways. Most
extremely and ultimately, one may be led to submit oneself faithfully to the utter mystery of God's ways, resting content with the

hope that there are good, albeit inscrutable, reasons why the world contains the misery it does.

Within the traditional framework, there are many solutions to the problem of evil: some say that every instance of evil either prevents a greater evil from occurring, or serves as a necessary precondition for a greater good; some say, alternatively, that evil is the human being's own making, and not God's doing, because God gave humans free will, and humans use this gift unwisely; some say that evil is God's just punishment for all of our crimes; some say that if there were no evil, then the concept of "good" would make no sense; some say that without evil, then there would be no resistance against which we could positively build our characters; some say that Satan is responsible, and not God. Common to all of these responses is an underlying assumption that the world is intelligible in principle, and that there is a reason for everything, even if it is a reason that God only knows.

As someone who did not recognize God's existence, Schopenhauer remained theoretically unmoved by the theistic formulations of the problem of evil. And yet he was not insensitive to the general philosophical desideratum to understand the nature of suffering, and was not intellectually content to accept evil as a brute fact. Among the various traditional solutions to the problem of evil, it is intriguing that Schopenhauer's understanding of the situation reflects one of the most austere traditional solutions, namely, that human beings themselves are the main culprits, and not God. This solution asserts that human beings are almost entirely responsible for evil, because, as noted above, God gave humans free will, and humans have chosen to use their God-given powers unwisely. Such an explanation, its defenders readily admit, does not account for natural evils such as disease, earthquakes, floods, and the like, but it goes a long way towards accounting for much of the pain humans experience: it is obvious that if people stopped harming each other as they have for millennia, the world would be a less threatening and more peaceful place in which to live.[6]

Schopenhauer's uncompromising view locates itself within the above intellectual sphere, for he claims that evil is mainly the result of human nature, reckoning that there is something truly diseased about the human being. Rather than associating human nature exclusively with free will, as is traditionally done, Schopenhauer goes a step further, and maintains that it is the rationalizing and will-pervaded human consciousness itself that is largely responsible for the world's evil. To understand this philosophical idea, it is important to recall that Schopenhauer's understanding of the human mind, although not his relatively negative assessment of it (which was Schopenhauer's own), was adopted in the main from Immanuel Kant (1724–1804). As we shall see, there is also much in Nietzsche that is Kantian.

According to both Kant and Schopenhauer, the rational human mind is not like a quiet mirror which immediately reflects that towards which it is aimed. It is more of an active processor: the mind actively organizes, and gives form to, sensory data directly presented to it, much as a computer organizes bits of electronic information into the readable form that appears on a computer screen. More specifically, the human mind is said to organize this sensory data – the materials of vision, hearing, touch, taste, smell – in a way that reflects the mind's own rational nature. And, according to Kant, it is the nature of the human mind to organize its sensory data both into a logical order, and into a sequential order in terms of space and time. Kant and Schopenhauer maintained that the world as it appears to us does not reflect how the world is "in itself," and that the way it appears within our human experience – as a causally-ordered world of individual things in space and in time – is partly, and yet ineradicably, due to the way we organize and inform what is given to us in sensation. For these two thinkers, there is more artificiality, artifactuality, and artistry in our perception of the world than is usually thought. To them, the world of daily experience is a synthetic product.

Kant's account of the human mind might sound common-sensical on first hearing, since computer-processing is now a familiar model that can retrospectively inform his eighteenth-century view, but as the implications and details of Kant's proposal are brought into close range, one's natural perspective is turned inside-out. To consider a simpler model for a moment, Kant's theory suggests that our minds are more like cookie-cutters that impress their form upon the "given" cookie-dough, rather than like mirrors that never touch what they reflect. He believed that his view was as philosophically revolutionary as the proposal that the observed daily movements of the stars and sun across the sky are not explained by referring to the intrinsic movements of those celestial bodies, but are explained in refer-ence to our own movement. As we now know, the observed movement of the sun across the sky each day is due to the spin-ning of the earth, just as the surrounding landscape appears to be spinning when one is on a merry-go-round.

Kant philosophically expanded upon this merry-go-round idea, claiming that the "out-there-ness" of things – that is, space itself – is also better understood by drawing an analogy to the movements of the sun and the stars: the world that appears to be "out there" he regarded as a construction of our own mental activity. He did acknowledge a foundational being that can be said to "be" quite independently of us, but the "out-there-ness" of this being, Kant believed, is an attribution projected from our own minds. For all we can know, he argued, the true Being – the "thing in itself" – could be independent of space and time, just as God is often thought to be independent of space and time.

A further analogy is useful here to convey Kant's central idea. Just as the experienced sweet taste of sugar is not "in" the sugar itself as it sits untasted in the sugarbowl on the kitchen table, the space, the time, the individual things which are all causally and scientifically connected to each other within our experience – in other words, the entire physical universe as we experience it, including human history itself, and including our bodies right here and now – do not, according to Kant, represent in a pure and transparent way the innermost reality of the way things are in themselves. We live in a world of "appearances" or "phenomena," he claims.

For Kant, the philosophical status of the world of daily experience, especially in reference to its dependable geometric and mathematical structure, is more analogous to the taste of sugar – a quality of human experience that arises internally when sugar crystals stimulate someone's tongue – than it is like the sugar crystals as they are in themselves, before they are tasted. Looking at an object in space is like tasting sugar – both involve experiences whose qualities are as much due to our own constitution as they are due to the constitution of whatever we happen to be tasting or looking at. Within Kant's view, this means, quite profoundly and also importantly with respect to a good portion of Nietzsche's views, that human beings are not in the position to know the exact nature of ultimate reality, even in principle. Every Kantian sees through a glass, very darkly, and they believe that everyone else's perception is similarly restricted.[7]

Strange to say, the human mind itself stands in the way of knowing the absolute truth on this Kantian position, because the human mind is finite, and must inform whatever it knows in its own particularly finite way. If one were only a tongue, so to speak, and were only in a position to know what sugar is by tasting it, then one would never be able to know what sugar is in itself, as it is independently of its being tasted. That dimension of the sugar would remain an eternal mystery for a being whose connection to the world was exclusively through the sense of taste. Just as the taste of sugar significantly reflects the structure of our tongues, perceived colors, in turn, reflect the structure of our eyes, and experienced sounds reflect the structure of our ears. Far more than is usually imagined, our perception of the world echoes our own modes of perception. Kant philosophically extends and deepens this basic idea, referring not especially to the superficial limits of our eyes, ears, and tongues, but to the limits of our very intellect, in conjunction with the limits of our spatial and temporal awareness.

Although Schopenhauer more optimistically believed that humans could know, or at least come close to knowing, the absolute truth, he agreed with Kant that the world of space and time is mostly a human construction, and that with respect to the way things are in themselves, independently of human existence, space and time do not necessarily apply. Reality in itself – what would remain if there were no humans – could be spaceless and timeless. Given this Kantian view of the human mind and of the world of human experience, the realm within which suffering occurs – the spatial and temporal world – becomes an artifact of human making, and a direct reflection of human nature's activity.

Schopenhauer, who accepts Kant's views on the nature of space and time, thus maintains that human beings are themselves the creators of evil in the world, insofar as their own minds express the general conditions through which evil is made possible. For him, the human mind structures raw fields of disjointed sensory data into a single world which contains individuals arranged across a spatial and temporal expanse. And if there were no individuals, then there would be no suffering. And if there were no humans, then there would be no individuals, so the Kantian theory suggests, since individuation is only a feature of our human way of connecting our consciousness to what is there independently of our existence.

At one point Schopenhauer describes our creation of our commonly experienced world as the "will" – that is, reality itself –

shining through our minds, as if our minds were a "magic lantern," and as if reality itself were a single, undivided light. The poetic beauty of the image notwithstanding, it conveys an appreciation of how Schopenhauer explains the existence of evil and why, moreover, he ultimately turns his attention away from the mundane world. He writes:

> Just as a magic lantern shows a multitude of different pictures, all of which are illuminated by one and the same flame, so it is within all of the manifold appearances which together fill the world, or which follow each other as events, that only *one will* appears, whose visibility the objectivity of everything is, and which remains unmoved throughout each change.[8]

The "magic lantern" is our mind that apprehends, as it expresses, the more encompassing universal will under the condition that this single will appears as fractured into innumerable objects that are distributed mosaically across space and time. The sands of time are, in effect, the sands of our own mindscape; the infinity of space, as far as can be known, is nothing more than an infinity projected by our own consciousness. Schopenhauer observes, quite painfully, that this renders the human mind responsible for constructing an appearance, or grand theater stage, that involves, for instance, animals fighting and eating each other, people warring against each other, innumerable harms, and virtually endless suffering. We human beings, on this Schopenhauerian vision of the world, by the virtue of our ability to organize diverse sensory data into individual things – by virtue of our original capacity to know anything at all – reveal ourselves to be monstrous playwrights who are the scene-setters of a terrifying vision. Such is the bitter fruit of knowledge. It is perhaps not a mere coincidence that Mary Shelley's novel, *Frankenstein*, was also published in 1818 – the same year as the publication of Schopenhauer's *The World as Will and Representation* – for they both associate humanity with monstrosity, especially in relation to those aspirations which involve the desire to become superhuman?

In connection with Schopenhauer's interpretation of Kant, one can say that Kant ascribes virtually godlike powers to the human being, for according to him, humans are the very creators of space and time. And as noted, Schopenhauer observes almost ironically that if humans are the creators of space and time, then they are the authors of a warlike scene: the infinity-projecting human nature gives birth to terror, one can say, just as the godlike aspirations of Dr. Frankenstein gave birth to a creature comparably imperfect. So it is not the misuse of free will that is responsible for evil, as some traditionalists claim. It is the very presence of rational human consciousness in its quest for knowledge. We have no choice but to generate evil, if, as Schopenhauer believes, the world itself is "will." For once the will is divided against itself, conflict arises. Which is to say that Schopenhauer regards the human condition as both awesome and awful, terrific and terrifying, for we seem to be condemned to both amaze and appall ourselves.

At the beginning of the nineteenth century, the less attractive aspects of the human being were becoming more explicitly thematized, and the raw, instinctual, amoral energies within us which Sigmund Freud (1856–1939) later referred to as the "id," or the "it," were beginning to emerge as a subject for reflection.[9] Peaceful beauty was giving way to breathtaking sublimity as the leading aesthetic value, and by the beginning of the twentieth century, sublimity and the awe-filled quality of experience gave way to the straightforwardly distorted and awful, at least when judged by the lights of neoclassical tastes. During Schopenhauer's time, however, such initial apprehensions of the irrational, disproportionate, and overwhelming were still being conveyed within a context where traditional morality maintained a strong psychological force, with the consequence that many of the monstrous apprehensions that were initially expressed remained set within a wider, more kindhearted, thematic – one where human history retained the quality of a morality play. Witness one of the earlier dawnings of the nihilistic mentality – one that Nietzsche would later consider with far more intestinal fortitude – expressed in the year 1800 by the German Idealist philosopher, Johann Gottlieb Fichte (1762–1814). Fichte formulated the following vision, only to reject this idea of a meaningless universe as psychologically unbearable:

> I should eat and drink, only in order to hunger and thirst again, and eat and drink, merely until the open grave under my feet swallows me up as a meal for the earth? Should I create more beings like myself, so that they can eat and drink and die, and so they can leave behind beings of their own, so that they can do the same as I have already done? What is the point of this continual, self-contained and ever-returning circle, this repetitive game that always starts again in the same way, in which everything is, in order to fade away, and fades away, only in order to return again as it was – this monster, continually devouring itself in order to reproduce itself, and reproduce itself, in order to devour itself?[10]

Fichte rejected the above ouroboric scene in favor of a more linear world-interpretation within which everything acts naturally, inevitably, and progressively towards a moral and harmonious end, even if this end is a perpetually long-distant one.[11] He was able to lift the veil from the possibility of a thoroughly meaningless world only for a moment's glimpse, and he needed to let the comforting prospect of a rational and meaningful world's-end drop quickly back into fundamental place. Schopenhauer held up this veil for a noticeably longer period of time, but he too eventually retreated into another kind of salvation, one that involved the dissolution of one's individuality and a flight into universal forms of consciousness. Nietzsche gazed at this "ceaseless and unvarying round" even longer, and after having allowed himself to become more deeply burned by the Medusa-like vision of paralyzing meaninglessness, fought to develop a more down-to-earth, existentially-centered view in recognition of such a threatening experience. Nietzsche's "yes" to life is none other than his fully fledged engagement with the self-propelling wheel of birth and death.

Schopenhauer, while accepting the Kantian position that humans are themselves responsible for the appearance of there being a multitude of objects in the world, did not follow Kant in regarding this as a morally neutral fact; Schopenhauer was viscerally repulsed by the productions and projections of his own human nature. For without the diverse objects of experience, there would be no fighting and no conflict. So Schopenhauer – known popularly as a "pessimist" – can be appreciated in his less-than-contented attitude, if we note how he regarded humans as being metaphysically diseased, since the very mechanism we must use to attain any knowledge at all produces a morally-disheartening experiential scene, namely that of a "dog eat dog" natural world which is thoroughly "red in tooth and claw." The scenario Fichte initially described is the very production of human nature itself, according to Schopenhauer. Nietzsche, apprehending the same vision, adopted an entirely different attitude towards the world's pain and violence, observing how such ostensibly negative aspects of the world can nonetheless sustain a positive value. In the end, though, he often drifted towards the conclusion that the human being is "human, all-too-human" and that it needed to be "overcome." Nietzsche loved to celebrate life, but he frequently had a very difficult time celebrating humanity.

Schopenhauer thus established a philosophical interpretation of the world where the idea of "life," as involving suffering, cannot be avoided in ordinary human experience. Not only is the core of reality on Schopenhauer's view a blind urge that is nothing more than unceasing want, the mind of the human being is considered to be a kaleidoscope of terror that multiply fractures the raw urge of reality and sets it against itself.[12] Since the individuated and dissociated will that "feasts on itself" is an appearance generated by the human being, Schopenhauer could not say "yes" to the analytic and dissecting human mind. He assigned all responsibility for the existence of individual suffering to the human being, and judged that human nature has a negative value. This is one of Schopenhauer's major points of difference with Nietzsche, who strove for a more positive interpretation of the human condition, although Nietzsche usually did so, not in reference to humanity as a whole, but in connection with particular individuals and particular types of individuals. Schopenhauer wrote:

> If one wants to know what people are worth, morally considered, in full and in general, one should consider their fate, in full and in general. This is privation, wretchedness, misery, agony and death. Eternal justice reigns; if they were not so generally despicable, then their fate, considered in general, would not be so pathetic. In this sense we can say: the world itself is the judiciary of the world. If one were to put all of the world's misery on one side of the scale, and all the world's guilt on the other, the pointer would be right at the center.[13]

The religious and philosophic question which Nietzsche inherited, then, is whether Schopenhauer was correct to ascribe a negative value to human life, even if human life involves great misery, and even if humans themselves are mostly to blame for their tragic condition. Nietzsche searched for an interpretation of the world-situation which did not require faith in God to justify the existing suffering – an interpretation within which one can nonetheless say "yes" to life, even though life might be miserable, and even though life might not be miserable merely in this or that instance, but fundamentally permeated with pain and disappointment, no matter what kind of life one lives.

Schopenhauer regarded the human being – in its condition of complete philosophical enlightenment and wisdom – as the bearer of all the world's suffering. A superhuman level of strength is thus required – virtually the strength of a god – to "affirm life," which is to say that, for Schopenhauer, the truth of the human condition is essentially unbearable: "According to the true nature of things, each person has as his own, all the suffering of the world, and must indeed consider all possible sufferings as actual for him, so long as he is the firm will to live, i.e., says 'yes' to life with his full strength."[14]

What we encounter here is an outlook suggesting that if we are to affirm life with all of our strength, we must become akin to the tortured Jesus, who is said to have taken upon himself all of the world's sins and suffering, all of its guilt, and all of its pain. If we intend to affirm life with all of our strength, we must be confident about having a virtually superhuman strength, lest we end up being crushed by the consequences of having said "yes" to life. Implicit in Schopenhauer's vision, then, is the thought that life-affirmation requires fortitude of a superhuman kind. Schopenhauer ultimately preferred peace of mind over the struggle to achieve a life-affirming attitude, and he advocated a withdrawal from life as a means to secure a transcendence of life's sufferings.

Schopenhauer's resulting conception of the human condition is noticeably dim, for he regarded individual human life as a very sad joke. He could not see the value in choosing to remain within its mundane constraints, and he yearned for alternative, extraordinary, and universalistic states of mind that provide a liberation from suffering, from wanting, from willing, from the world of individuals in conflict; he yearned for states of mind that induce a profound distancing from the unbearable stage upon which the tragicomedy of life transpires. He sought to transcend human nature itself. Hence, at the endpoint of Schopenhauer's view, we find him opting for the ascetic life of renunciation and "life negation," for he believed that once one apprehends the truth of the human situation, the idea of affirming life and humanity becomes repulsive and devastating. In short, Schopenhauer sought for some potent spiritual relief from this tragic world.

Consider, in sharp contrast, a passage from the beginning of Nietzsche's *Thus Spoke Zarathustra* (1883–85) – a passage that reads almost as if it could be Nietzsche (as Zarathustra) conversing with Schopenhauer (as the saint):

> Zarathustra climbed down from the mountains alone, encountering no one. But when he came into the forest, there stood before him a venerable old man, who had left his holy hut to look for roots in the forest. And thus the old man spoke to Zarathustra:
>
> "This wanderer is not an unknown to me: many years ago he went by here. Zarathustra he was called; but he has changed.
>
> At that time you carried your ashes to the mountains: will you now carry your fire into the valleys? Don't you fear to be punished as a fire-starter?
>
> Yes, I recognize Zarathustra. Pure are his eyes, and his mouth betrays no disgust. Does he not walk along like a dancer?
>
> Zarathustra is a changed man, Zarathustra has turned into a child, Zarathustra is an awakened-one: what do you want then, with those who are asleep?
>
> As in the sea, you lived in solitude, and the sea carried you. Well now, you want to climb up onto the land? Well now, you want to drag your body along again?"
>
> Zarathustra answered, "I love people."
>
> "Why," said the holy man, "did I go into the forest and into isolation? Was it not because I loved people so very much?[15]
>
> Now, I love God: the people I do not love.[16] The human being is for me a too-imperfect thing. Loving people would kill me."[17]

Drawing the respective correspondences to Schopenhauer and Nietzsche from the above characters, we can regard the saint as a person who, after having, Jesus-like, assumed the burden of the world's suffering, found the vision of humanity's truth too much for a finite person to bear. Hence, the "love of people" would kill the saint if he remained within that down-to-earth world. Drinking from this fountain would poison his sensitive soul. In contrast, Zarathustra embodies Nietzsche's dissatisfaction with such a seemingly escapist, ascetic, and superficially holy alternative, for Zarathustra intends to remain in a condition of "loving" the human being – a condition which entails "affirming life" rather than denying it.[18] And indeed, the saint, given his moral commitments, retreats from life with maybe good reason: the prospect of being obliged to forgive unconditionally and with pure, unselfish love the heartless murderers of one's own children and relatives – forgiving the unforgivable – could be too much of an affront to an ordinary person's sense of justice.[19]

This general theme of "the struggle to affirm life" directly in the face of its pains permeates most of Nietzsche's writings. In such reflections, he battles with traditional Christian morality, and eventually rejects it outright, not so much to preserve his sense of justice, but to preserve his sense of bodily and spiritual health. His antagonism towards some traditional reactions to life's ills, which he interpreted as prescribing an escapist attitude, is centered in his conviction that it is of absolute importance to remain completely down-to-earth and in contact with experienced reality and with life itself. Living in denial of life's ills conflicts with his philosophical urge to be true to life. Nietzsche did his best to refrain from all spiritual anaesthetics, striving to gain in character by directly "toughing" life out.

2

The worship
of wildlife

Nietzsche's university studies in classical philology were so impressive that he was awarded a doctoral degree without being obliged to submit a formal dissertation. He was then – in an extraordinary achievement for a twenty-four-year-old – immediately appointed to a professorial position in Switzerland at the University of Basel. Nietzsche's brilliance was evident, and as his colleagues eagerly awaited the publication of his first extended academic study, his own aspirations motivated him to write a book intended to be of long-lasting interest.

Many years later, Nietzsche observed about himself that some people are born posthumously, and this is what happened with his first book, *The Birth of Tragedy* (1872). It is read today as an inspired account of early Greek tragedy, but it did not enjoy success during Nietzsche's lifetime. The book was warmly received with supportive enthusiasm by Richard Wagner and his limited circle, but as a work which aimed to establish Nietzsche's solid reputation within the international field of academic philology, it was a professional disappointment: the short volume was too speculative, too filled with diverse themes, and too visionary for the times. It initially drew scathing criticism from some members of his profession, and was thereafter left alone quietly in relative neglect.[20]

Although *The Birth of Tragedy* is manifestly concerned with the origins of Greek tragedy, Nietzsche approached his subject synoptically.[21] Thinking in very broad terms, he first considered the general characteristics of Greek culture at the time of tragedy's emergence as an art form. Then, looking back into the history of the Greeks to those peoples who were their predecessors, he developed general hypotheses about the Greeks' overall psychology and metaphysical perceptions, using all of this to ground speculative projections about where we, as members of modern civilization, stand in relationship to the classical Greek culture and the experience of Greek tragedy. The subject matter of Nietzsche's first book extended far beyond the details of Greek tragedy, for it provided a general understanding of the ancient Greeks as they reflect upon modern society. He sought nothing less than to make his studies practically and culturally relevant to everyone in his contemporary European civilization.

Why, though, would someone who aspired to write a culturally influential book focus upon the esoteric topic of ancient Greek tragedy? Given Nietzsche's historical situation and interests, Greek tragedy was less esoteric than it now appears, and was far more attractive than one might suspect. First of all, although comedy appears in many cultures, the tragic art form appears to have been a uniquely Greek phenomenon, so given its stature within cultural history in general, it is a reasonable place for a person who studied classical Greek culture, as Nietzsche did, to devote his or her energies.

Second, during Nietzsche's time, there had been a revival of interest in Greek culture among those who discerned in the Greeks an extraordinarily healthy quality that might therapeutically be transplanted into a contemporary European culture in spiritual crisis. The prevailing opinion, at least among many intellectuals, was that the contemporary culture was sick and weak, and that it needed a rejuvenating shot in the arm. Organized Christianity was becoming less and less inspiring, and the increasing mechanization and dehumanization of the working population in the ever-growing world of factories and mass-production facilities was slowly turning people into mere appendages of money-making machines. Nietzsche himself never tired of condemning the business-and-bureaucracy-related values of the "market place," and with it, the capitalist values that reinforced the beliefs – even in the sphere of morality – that people should always "be paid" for their deeds, and that God is a kind of supreme paymaster.[22]

Third, the particular influence of Schopenhauer's avant-garde outlook on Nietzsche had implanted the idea that life can be perceived as fundamentally tragic. So Nietzsche realized that an investigation of the Greek experience of tragedy-as-art could illuminate the nature of life, in a way that harmonized with a philosophy that, as we can now see in retrospect, was at the cutting edge.

Fourth, since the performance of Greek tragedy took place during the springtime and in connection with life-celebrating festivals in honor of the god Dionysus, there is a close relationship between the "birth of tragedy" and the affirmation of life and health – themes that Nietzsche wished to advocate in reaction to, and as a more hopeful advance upon, Schopenhauer's opposing tendency towards life negation, or "denial of the will."

The feral Dionysus and the beautiful Apollo

Nietzsche constructed *The Birth of Tragedy* around two complementary and creative energies, whose interaction he believed was crucial to the emergence of Greek tragedy and the best of Greek culture in general. These can be described as "wildlife" (or "feral" or "animal") energies on the one hand, and "idealizing" (or "intellectualizing" or "perfecting") energies on the other. Nietzsche referred to the feral energies as "Dionysian," and to the idealizing energies as "Apollonian," associating them, respectively, with the states of frenzied intoxication and angelic dreaming. This distinction was partly inspired by Schopenhauer's theory of art, where the arts divide into the more willful art of music, which Schopenhauer maintained was a direct copy of reality itself, and the more contemplative plastic/verbal arts, which Schopenhauer maintained led to a tranquil awareness of timeless Ideas, understood as the underlying ideal patterns of the daily world.

With the main art forms of classical Greece in mind, Nietzsche coordinated the Apollonian energies with the art of sculpture and the Dionysian energies with the art of music. At a more philosophical level, these Apollonian and Dionysian creative energies paralleled Schopenhauer's distinction between the world's experiential surface, which appears to us as a set of individual things distributed throughout space and time, as opposed to the world's innermost heart, as it is in its spaceless and timeless self. Apollo represented the composed, ordered, controlled, safe, sanitized, perfected, and beautiful world of illusion, and Dionysus represented the wild, disordered, unmanageable, essentially horrific world of raw, chance-driven, accidental, brutal reality itself. Nietzsche summarized the relationships between these ideas and Schopenhauer's theory of art in the following:

> In contrast to all who are keen to derive the arts from a single principle, as the necessary inspiring-force to every work of art, I would like to hold in view each of the two artistic divinities of the Greeks, Apollo and Dionysus, and recognize in their living and perceptual representations, *two* artworlds that differ from each other in their deepest essence and highest goals. Apollo stands before me as the transfiguring genius of the *principii individuationis* [principle of individuation], through which alone, redemptive release by means of illusion is to be achieved; whereas through Dionysus's mystical cry of jubilation, the spell of individuation is broken, and the way to the mothers of being, to the innermost kernel of things, is laid open. This awesome tension, which opens gapingly between the plastic arts, as Apollonian, and music, as the Dionysian art, has been

revealed to only one of the great thinkers, to the extent that he, without the guidance of the Hellenic divinities' symbolization, bestowed upon music a different character and a different source than all the other arts, because it is not, like the others, a reflection of appearances, but an immediate reflection of the Will itself, and therefore represents what is metaphysical with respect to everything physical in the world, and represents the thing in itself, with respect to appearances. (Schopenhauer, *Welt als Wille und Vorstellung*, I, p. 310.) [the reference here to Schopenhauer is Nietzsche's own][23]

Nietzsche bestows much credit upon Schopenhauer in this excerpt, but we should note that since the end of the 1700s in Germany, there had already been a prevailing "Apollonian" conception of Greek culture – one that had been initiated by the ground-breaking art historian, Johann Winckelmann (1717–68). Both Nietzsche and Schopenhauer inherited Winckelmann's conception of the Greeks as expressive of a "noble simplicity and tranquil grandeur" and Nietzsche complemented the prevalent peaceful, calm, reason-abiding conception with an emphasis on the more unruly, life-centered, non-rational, and instinctual Dionysian energies. For Nietzsche, the classical Greeks were not only a beautiful people; they were a fundamentally instinct-driven people, and he believed that their naturalness and intensely free expression of emotion was largely responsible for their supreme psychological health.[24]

Nietzsche thus coordinated the Schopenhauerian "appearance vs. reality" distinction with his own "Apollonian vs. Dionysian" distinction. And since Schopenhauer claimed that the world is "will," and that this will is, most importantly, the "will-to-live," Nietzsche regarded the Dionysian energies as fundamentally life energies, and moreover, as energies associated with a hard-to-bear truth about life: injury, conflict, appropriation, exploitation, and pain are unavoidable.[25] To be born into this world is, among many other things, to be exposed to pain. With such a theory in hand,

Nietzsche associated the idea of "life" with the ideas of reality, existence, and truth. To experience the truth – which, for him, was harsh, dangerous, sexual, and animalistic – is to experience the Dionysian, feral quality of experience.

As an indication of what these Dionysian energies are like, without tempering or control by the rationalizing and idealizing Apollonian energies, we can consider the following excerpt:

> From all corners of the ancient world from Rome to Babylon – leaving aside here the modern world – we can certify the existence of festivals, whose type is related to that of the Greeks, in the best case, as the bearded satyr, to which the goat lent its name and attributes, is related to Dionysus himself. In almost every case, the center of the festivals resided in an overflowing sexual unrestraint, whose waves washed away all social integrity and its venerable constitution; the wildest beastlike urges of nature were here unleashed to the point of that horrible mixture of voluptuousness and cruelty, which always seemed to me to be the real "witches'-brew." Against these feverish stirrings of these festivals, whose knowledge pressed upon the Greeks from all land and sea routes, it appears that for a time they were completely secured and protected through the proud figure of Apollo, who held up the Medusa's head to this power that was as dangerous as could be, to this grotesque, barbaric, Dionysian force. It is in Doric art, that the majestic and repelling figure of Apollo is eternalized.[26]

In their free and unleashed form, the Dionysian energies are dangerous, grotesque, cruel, sexual, instinctual, and savage. They are the hardcore energies of life and of the jungle, and for Nietzsche, at this time at least, a world ruled exclusively by such energies – upon reflection – is difficult to welcome and embrace. Under the turbulent domination of such a Medusa, existence itself seems to be alien and meaningless, because one is born only to eat and be eaten, either violently by beings like oneself, or slowly by the erosion of time's mere passing.

What we have before us in Nietzsche's untempered, Dionysian vision of the world is what Fichte and Schopenhauer described as the endless conflictual, day-to-day world, where the will constantly "feasts upon itself," and where animals and people fight each other in their ultimately futile efforts towards self-preservation. And yet, unlike Schopenhauer and many thinkers of his time, Nietzsche was not thoroughly intimidated and disheartened by this vision to the point of disgust, embittered cynicism, and retreat. He regarded it as horrific, but he fought to interpret life in a way that would allow him to revel in it nonetheless, as someone who could dwell in the energetic and oceanic thrill of "life itself," despite its frightfully intimidating aspects.

European culture in decline

Consonant with most European thinkers during the late eighteenth and nineteenth centuries, Nietzsche adored classical Greek culture as an example of exceptional human health, and he sang among the chorus of those who longed for a resurrection of the Greek spirit. He estimated the quality of his own time accordingly, upholding the Greek ideal as a measuring stick. Using the distinction between "Dionysian" and "Apollonian" energies as his instrument, he claimed that in pre-Greek times, the feral Dionysian energies overshadowed the more composed Apollonian energies, and that cultural groups remained relatively animalistic and unrefined. In classical Greek times, the Dionysian and Apollonian energies became, as he saw it, optimally balanced, so as to allow the Greeks to develop their instinctual energies in a natural and creative manner, without being completely and crudely ruled by them. In post-Greek times, Dionysian energies supposedly became submerged, repressed, and unhealthily overshadowed by rationalistic, idealizing, Apollonian energies.[27] Rationality, Nietzsche believed, became a force of spiritual suppression, almost to the

point of smothering human vitality. Contrary to traditional thinking in the West, Nietzsche denied that human nature is to be
equated with rational nature, and he was convinced that the classical definition of the human being as a "rational animal" overly
affirmed rationality as the supposedly "best" part of the human
being. He saw this classical definition as downplaying the power of
instinct, and hence as subordinating to rationality, the driving
power of life itself.

According to Nietzsche, the consequence has been that ever
since the times of the later classical Greeks, Western civilization
has grown increasingly weak due to its over-reliance on rationalistic thinking – a mode of thinking that Nietzsche traced back to
the influence of Socrates (*c.* 470–399 BC), and what some histori-
ans mark, with quite a different evaluation, as the eminent beginnings of Western philosophical culture. Socrates has long been
regarded as the patron saint of Western philosophy, but for
Nietzsche the classical philologist, Socrates remained an ambivalent figurehead. He could see how Socratic super-rationality
could be toxic when taken in large doses, and how it could also be
addictive. Concerning the present-day situation, he said:

> Our entire modern world… recognizes the theory-driven person
> – of whom Socrates is the archetype and forefather – as the ideal,
> as someone who is armed with the highest powers of knowledge,
> and who works in the service of science. All of our educational
> strategies have essentially this ideal in view; every other type of
> existence has to drag itself up from the sidelines, as a merely
> permitted, and not really desired, type.[28]

Resonating within this century-old observation is an attitude
still encountered in some quarters – one which, ironically, is
hardly Socratic. It is often expressed as the prescription to make
one's professional vocation "financially profitable," "practical," and
something one can "do" to gain observably material rewards. In

this light, it is easier to appreciate some of Nietzsche's uneasiness with exclusively pragmatic and business-oriented mentalities, especially in their more unrefined versions.

Nietzsche's understanding of his present-day situation, his continual attacks on Christianity, his questioning of "truth," his challenge to traditional forms of morality, his caustic criticisms of the majority of his contemporaries, his feeling of having been born out of step with the times in which he lived, his sense of needing to offer some kind of therapy to the people of his time – all of this – can be understood in light of his conception of the decline of Greek culture, and the later emergence and subsequent domination of narrowly technological and utility-oriented styles of thinking. Nietzsche is less critical of Socrates himself than he is of the rationalistic tradition which Socrates helped to precipitate. Stated more affirmatively, many themes within Nietzsche's outlook can be grasped in light of his understanding of the healthy quality of classical Greek culture, and in particular, in reference to Greek tragedy, which was grounded less in abstract reasoning and far more on the direct experience of instinctual energies.

Greek tragedy as a transcendence-festival

What did Nietzsche find valuable in the tragic art of the Greeks? For him, Greek tragedy afforded an awareness of life that acknowledged the suffering he perceived daily life to embody, while at the same time, it offered some protection from this vision – a protection that allowed one to perceive the truth about life without falling into a condition of hopelessness and despair. Nietzsche maintained that the experience of tragedy provided a healthy balance: by incorporating an Apollonian temperament into the scene, it softly polished the Dionysian passions, desires, and devouring appetites with a sense of perfection, such that the Dionysian life-energies neither ran rampant in a devastating, cannibalistic frenzy, nor were unhealthily repressed, as supposedly happened in later years and subsequent cultures. The experience of Greek tragedy was akin to beholding the Medusa's face not directly, but in the reflection of Perseus's shield of wisdom.

Nietzsche maintained that the experience of Greek tragedy offered a "metaphysical consolation": it conveyed the idea that although we, as individuals, struggle and suffer in life and eventually die, from a more magnificent perspective we are part of "life itself" and our participation in that life is our true, joyous, thrilling, and eternal being. As some Christians find solace in the prospect of participation in an otherworldly kingdom of God after their bodies die, Nietzsche found solace in the possibility of participating in the universal life forces that permeate the here-and-now, earthly world of the living. Nietzsche exalted life in its concrete, down-to-earth manifestations. He regarded the metaphysical comfort associated with the oceanic blending of oneself into life itself as arising not so much from the idea that suffering is eliminated (although this accounted for part of the comfort), but from the perception of ourselves as participants in a powerful universal energy, as being part of the epic-scale dance of life, and hence, from the perception of ourselves as everlasting beings. One of the comforts of this experience is the feeling that we have transcended our finitude and death as individuals, because at this level of universal awareness we become "primordial being itself" during our earthly lives:

> Also, Dionysian art wants to convince us of the eternal thrill [*der ewigen Lust*[29]] of existence: we ought to seek out this thrill, not in the appearances, but behind them. We should recognize how everything that arises, has to be prepared for a painful descent, as it looks into the horror of individual existence – while also not allowing itself to be turned into stone: a metaphysical consolation

momentarily tears us away from the movements of the changing configurations. We are really for a brief moment the primordial being itself and experience its unbridled craving and thrill for existence; the struggle, the anguish, the annihilation of appearances, strikes us now as a necessity, in view of the overflow of uncountable forms of existence that are pressing and pushing themselves into life, in view of the excessively fertile productiveness of the world-will. At the same time, we are pierced by the fierce thorns of this anguish, where we simultaneously become unified with the unrelenting, primordial thrill of existence, and where we, in Dionysian rapture, have an inkling of the indestructibility and eternity of this thrill.[30]

In the same way, I believe, the Greek person of culture felt himself self-dissolvingly uplifted in view of the chorus of satyrs: and this is the most immediate effect of Dionysian tragedy, that the state and society, and above all, the distances between each and every person, dissolve into a powerful feeling of oneness, leading right to the heart of nature. The metaphysical consolation – with which, as I have already here pointed out – is that life is at the ground of things, and that despite all changes of appearances, it is invincibly powerful and filled with gusto. This consolation appears in bodily clarity as the chorus of satyrs, which is a chorus of natural beings, living on behind all civilization, indivisibly, and despite all changes of generation and histories of peoples, remaining eternally the same.

With this chorus the profound and sensitive Greeks – people who were capable of the deepest suffering – consoled themselves, as they gazed dashingly into the horribly destructive tendency of so-called world-history, and into the gruesome cruelty of nature; in danger of yearning for a Buddhistic negation of the will, art saves them, and through art, life saves them.[31]

In truth, though, that hero is the suffering Dionysus of the Mysteries, the god who experiences in himself the sufferings of individuation – the god of whom wonderful myths tell how, as a lad, he was ripped to shreds by the Titans, and how he was worshipped in this condition as Zagreus… In these observations we have already the elements of a profound and pessimistic world-outlook, together at the same time with *the mystery-teachings of tragedy*: the foundational knowledge of the oneness of all which exists, the recognition of individuation as the ultimate source of distress,[32] and art as the joyful hope, that the spell of individuation can be broken, as the divination of a reinstituted oneness.[33]

In these crucial excerpts, Nietzsche associates the god Dionysus with life in general and with the individual manifestations of life in their mutual struggles against one another. He also refers to the individuation, or fragmentation, of life energies as "the primal cause of evil," and, in related excerpts, as "the origin and primal cause of all suffering" and as "something objectionable in itself." In Schopenhauerian terms, Nietzsche's *Dionysus-as-a-whole* represents the Schopenhauerian "will-to-live" in general, and Nietzsche's *Dionysus-as-dismembered* represents the struggling and fighting individuals who, as manifestations of life itself, each suffer and die. The entire cosmos is personified as the being of Dionysus, in one or the other of his aspects. Dionysus is the Nietzschean Leviathan.

The "metaphysical comfort" provided by the experience of Greek tragic art is the experience of world-transcendence: it involves a transition in consciousness from the narrow standpoint of the struggling and self-defensive individual, to the expanded standpoint of the universal life energies, which Nietzsche maintains are eternally joyous, exuberantly fertile, ecstatic, creative, powerful, and pleasurable. Nietzsche believes, in effect, that the art of Greek tragedy displays for us on the theatrical stage a vision of the world whose articulated, individualized, fragmented, and ever-changing surface is terrible, and whose unified, universal, and eternal depth is thrillingly joyous. It is a vision wherein the individuals in the former realm can transform their perspective from a more individualistic to a more universal outlook, and thereby achieve a measure of metaphysical satisfaction and release from suffering.[34]

The extent to which Schopenhauer's philosophy influenced Nietzsche has remained a matter of debate among scholars, with some claiming that Nietzsche never fully broke away from Schopenhauer, others claiming that Nietzsche arrived at his own characteristic views midway through his career, at about the time of his book, *Daybreak* (1880), and still others claiming that Schopenhauer's views took only a brief, youthful hold on Nietzsche, only to appear insignificantly in *The Birth of Tragedy* (1872). Such diversity of opinion notwithstanding, it is clear that at the outset of his career, Nietzsche departed from the spirit of Schopenhauer's philosophy insofar as he tried to affirm life, rather than to negate it, even though he retained much of the conceptual framework of Schopenhauer's vision.

It is generally accepted that, in contrast to Schopenhauer, Nietzsche offered a more "life-affirming" view in *The Birth of Tragedy*. This is true, however, in only a restricted sense: if we attend closely to the conception of life that Nietzsche affirmed, we see that he did not affirm life in its ordinary, day-to-day condition – a condition where life is articulated into a set of individuals that stand in essential disharmony and conflict. Nietzsche, like Schopenhauer and Fichte, regarded the unpolished vision of life as an almost unbearable jungle-scene, and at this intermediate stage in his intellectual development, he appears to have veiled this unnerving spectacle in order to make it more psychologically manageable. He did not fully affirm ordinary life in its horrific determinacy; rather, he immersed himself in the more abstracted, generalized idea of "life in general," defined in a way that kept it relatively remote from the particular sufferings of daily life.

Nietzsche admitted that suffering is necessary as an expression of life, but his metaphysical ecstasy issued only when he transcended the individual standpoint and assumed the perspective of "the *one* living being, with whose creative joy [one is] united." He followed Schopenhauer closely, insofar as he maintained that all suffering arises due to the principle of individuation, which is to say that Nietzsche's solution to the problem of evil matched Schopenhauer's: in our ordinary state of mind, we individuate things, and our suffering arises within this condition of human-created individuation, but when we transcend our own individuality and our individuating-mentality, then evil dissolves, and shows itself to be an illusion. The difference between the two is that Schopenhauer identified a state of non-individuation located metaphysically beyond the world altogether, whereas Nietzsche characterized a state of non-individuation that is more earth-centered, and that is accessible as the awareness of universal "life itself" in Dionysic ecstasy.

The "affirmation of life" via tragic art in Nietzsche's *The Birth of Tragedy* was directly inspired by Schopenhauer's account of aesthetic experience, since this experience is said to lift us out of the suffering-infused world of space and time. This is easily understandable, since the experience of tragic art is, on the face of things, an aesthetic experience. What is peculiar about Nietzsche's account is that in the experience of tragic art, our awareness is not transported to a realm of timeless Ideas, but to a realm more closely aligned with what Schopenhauer described in his account of moral awareness: for Nietzsche, tragic art transports us into the heart of life, where we become one with all living beings. Nietzsche regarded this condition as joyously thrilling, because awareness is expanded beyond its ordinary boundaries, and because all suffering supposedly arises from the principle of individuation which, at this level of universal awareness, is a principle left behind. Schopenhauer believed that the level of universal awareness wherein one identifies with "life in general" (that is, moral awareness) involves the dawning awareness of all suffering, since one thus identifies with every suffering being simultaneously. Each philosopher experienced the heart of life very differently, with Nietzsche experiencing a greater thrill, and with Schopenhauer experiencing a greater torture.

Since the states of mind described here are extraordinary, it is difficult to determine whose experience (if either) of the "heart of life," Nietzsche's or Schopenhauer's, is closer to the actual truth. It remains that Nietzsche's conception of the state of mind arising when one identifies with "life in general," unlike Schopenhauer's conception of moral awareness, involves a reduction of suffering, since he maintained that suffering itself arises as a result of the principle of individuation. It appears, then, that in his account of the aesthetic experience of tragedy Nietzsche removes the pain from what Schopenhauer described as "moral awareness," since he claimed that what we are aware of in the experience of tragedy is the will-to-life itself – the very content that Schopenhauer associates with the object of moral awareness. Although Nietzsche intended to develop a life-affirming view in *The Birth of Tragedy*, his conception of life-affirmation bears close affinities to the more escapist aesthetic and ascetic modes of consciousness that Schopenhauer described as transcending, rather than directly facing, the world of daily life.[35]

The rebirth of tragedy in Nietzsche's Germany

Classical Greek tragedy, according to Nietzsche, presents a balanced vision of our world: we apprehend the suffering of finite individuals, while we are comforted in becoming aware of the underlying, eternal delight inherent in life itself. As noted, he also believed that from the time of Socrates until his own century, this healthy vision had been disturbed, and that an over-rationalized, life-repressing attitude – an attitude that he referred to peculiarly as "optimism" – had taken over.[36] Living in the midst of what he considered to be an "optimistic" culture whose life forces had been devitalized by an overdose of logical and scientific thinking, Nietzsche looked hopefully for indications that the Greek spirit could be resurrected, and he found them in the German philosophy which had personally inspired him, namely, that of Kant and Schopenhauer. He also found these indications in the German music of his good friend and father-figure, Richard Wagner, among others. Witness the nationalistic tone of the following excerpts. It is a young, twenty-eight-year-old Nietzsche speaking, at a time long before he would decide that the Germans are "too full of beer" to be located at the leading edge of European culture.

> Out of the Dionysian foundation of the German spirit a power has risen up, which, having nothing in common with the original conditions of the Socratic culture, and from the standpoint of that culture is unable to be further explained or excused, and moreover, is in the eyes of that culture something horrible and incomprehensible, as well as overpowering and hostile: *German music*, in the way we should understand it, namely, in its powerful sunlike procession from Bach to Beethoven, and from Beethoven to Wagner.[37]

> Through the colossal bravery and wisdom of *Kant* and *Schopenhauer*, the most difficult victory has been won – the victory over the optimism that lies hidden in the essence of logic, and in turn, at the foundation of our culture. Although this optimism was believed to have discerned and penetrated all of the universe's riddles, as it was supported by completely unobjectionable eternal verities – ones where space, time and causality were regarded as fully unconditional, universally valid laws – Kant revealed how these, in fact, apply only to mere appearances, the work of *maya*. This optimism raises appearances to the level of the single and true reality, locating them at the innermost and true core of things, thus rendering impossible the real knowledge of this reality; i.e., as in the words of Schopenhauer, allowing the dreamer to sleep even more soundly.

This knowledge initiates a culture which I dare to call a tragic one, whose most important feature is that wisdom replaces science as the highest goal. This wisdom, unmoved by the seductive distractions of the sciences, turns with a steadfast eye towards the total world picture, and tries to grasp, with sympathetic feelings of love, the eternal suffering as its own suffering.[38]

Where does the mystery of this unity between German music and German philosophy point, if not towards a new form of existence, whose content we are able to discern for ourselves only from the Hellenic analogies? ... the feeling lives in us that the birth of a tragic age for the German spirit is only a return of that spirit to itself – a glorious self-rediscovery – after having been forced to live for so long in servitude, in a helpless barbarism, under the forms of enormous outside powers. Now, finally, with its own homecoming, it can dare to walk along before all other peoples, boldly and freely, without the apron-strings of a Romanesque civilization: if only it can constantly learn from a single people, from whom to learn anything, is a high honor and a distinct rarity.[39]

The musical greatness of Bach, Beethoven, and Wagner remains unquestionable to this day, and Kant's philosophy momentously redirected the history of Western philosophy. To "make room for faith," Kant narrowed the scope of provable knowledge, and indirectly stimulated in later thinkers alternative, provocative, and philosophically innovative efforts to attain knowledge of "absolute truth". In the philosophers who criticized Kant, but who also inevitably followed in his footsteps, these efforts relied not on the reasoning powers Kant had so effectively defined and circumscribed, but on analysis-resistant intuition and direct insight. In Nietzsche's estimation, Kant and Schopenhauer were among the first philosophers in the modern age who placed clear limits on the views of the Enlightenment, or "Age of Reason," in general and on the scientific enterprise in particular – an enterprise that stemmed from the optimism of the 1600s and 1700s, grounded on the belief that reason alone could resolve the riddles of the universe and secure a harmonious society on earth.

What is less solidly supported in *The Birth of Tragedy* is Nietzsche's unqualified belief that the spirit of Western culture would be resurrected through the German spirit, chiefly through the multi-media musical festivals of Richard Wagner. Both of these objects of Nietzsche's early admiration – Germany and Wagner – diminished in importance as his career progressed, but one idea from his early reflections on tragedy continued to extend throughout his writings. This is Nietzsche's antagonism to excessive and exclusively rationalistic thinking, to any science devoid of art, to any purely literalistic, non-literary, non-poetic approach to understanding the world, and to any conception of knowledge that neglects the importance of wisdom. Nietzsche associated the world of Greek tragedy with the world of myth, and he claimed that in order to grasp the full truth of things, one needs to think imaginatively, in mythic terms:

> He who recalls the immediate consequences of this restlessly progressing spirit of science will realize at once that *myth* was annihilated by it, and that, because of this annihilation, poetry was driven like a homeless being from her natural ideal soil. If we have been right in assigning to music the power of again giving birth to myth, we may similarly expect to find the spirit of science on the path where it inimically opposes this mythopoeic power of music.[40]

> The myth wants to be experienced vividly as a unique example of a universality and truth that gaze into the infinite.[41]

The question of whether or not Nietzsche fundamentally rejected the concept of "truth" is marked by extended controversy. A straightforward and elementary philosophical difficulty resides in rejecting the idea of truth altogether, for if one asserts without qualification that "there is no truth," then one has asserted a truth and has thereby accepted the idea of truth.[42]

Nietzsche sometimes tripped and fell into this logical indelicacy. At other times, he was careful to reject only specific ways to approach the truth, often including among these the purely literal-minded, direct, and logical ways. Nietzsche had his own scientific and literalistic moments, but he tended to regard the "neutrally observe and carefully measure" method of inquiry as too unrefined and insensitive to the many nuances of experience, and as being especially blind to the "behind-the-scenes" (e.g., the unconscious) reasons for why we assert, or believe, what we do. For Nietzsche, being too fiercely logical is a recipe for intellectual self-deadening and self-imposed ignorance. When searching for the most profound and far-reaching truths, he usually chose poetry before mathematics, and practical wisdom before mere book knowledge.

In the majority of his writings, Nietzsche held that the exclusively literalistic approach towards truth harbors an illusion because, by and large, he believed the truth cannot be reached in "a direct manner."[43] In one of his most famous prefaces, written fourteen years after *The Birth of Tragedy*, Nietzsche gave voice to this idea, using the same images he employed in his first book. Specifically, he said once more in *Beyond Good and Evil* (1886) that if one is interested in truth, then one's approach must be subtle and indirect. One way to achieve this end is to be metaphorically-minded; another way (as Nietzsche later conceived of himself) is to be a "physiologist" or "psychologist" who considers the unconscious reasons why people say what they do. It is here, in the less-manifest desires that remain mostly hidden to us, where Nietzsche believed we will often unfold the truth. To express this idea, he wrote the following in his preface to *Beyond Good and Evil*:

> Let us presuppose that the truth … is a woman. Then what? Are there not grounds to suspect that all philosophers, insofar as they were dogmatists, understood women rather badly? That the awful

seriousness, the awkward intrusiveness, with which they have hith-
erto approached truth, using such crude and rude methods, will
really work to capture a woman? What is certain is that she has let
no one capture her – and every type of dogmatism today stands
there distressed and disheartened, assuming it is still standing at all!
For there are those mockers who maintain that it has indeed
fallen, that all dogmatism is on the ground, and more, that all
dogmatism is taking its last breaths.

Seriously speaking, though, there are good reasons to believe,
that all philosophic dogmatism, so solemn, so ultimately valid it has
made itself out to be, may have nonetheless been only a noble
child's-play and the gropings of a beginner.[44]

Nietzsche refers above to philosophical "dogmatists" – those who
develop elaborate systems of thought and assert that the absolute
truth is captured by their conceptual system of interpretation.
With a challenging eye, he critically evaluated such attempts at
traditional philosophizing by examining them through his own
special lens, namely, "through the perspective of life." He considered them in reference to the kind of physiology the philosopher
happens to have, the kind of psychological desires that the person
has hidden, the kind of environment in which the person lives, and
what benefits the person obtains by accepting such a belief system.

This life-grounded style of evaluation is one way to approach
the truth "indirectly," insofar as it stands opposed to what is manifestly said, and to the extent that it considers the underlying motivations for the assertions themselves. Such is the tone of a good
deal of Nietzsche's later style of analysis, which we find embodied
in his notion of "genealogy."[45] In *The Birth of Tragedy*, there are the
seeds of this "indirect" approach to truth, to the extent that
Nietzsche contested the Socratic, rationalistic approach to the
world, and the assumption that the truth is to be found in the
straightforward, direct, literal, face value of an expression (i.e., as
would be presented in scientific formulas). By advocating this

indirect, poetic approach to truth, Nietzsche fashioned himself as suitable to be knowledge's true lover, and as a genuine philosopher in the literal sense of the word.

Truth, from the perspective of life

One year after the publication of *The Birth of Tragedy*, Nietzsche composed an essay entitled "On Truth and Lie in a Morally-Disengaged Sense" which, although it remained unpublished, is an instructive exemplar of Nietzsche's style of thought. In his first book, Nietzsche examined Greek culture through "the perspective of life," and this general idea of examining a subject matter, not from an absolute, "God's-eye" standpoint, but from some set of limited, realistic, finite, and human standpoints, he later developed as his doctrine of "perspectivism." This perspectivistic style of thought is one of Nietzsche's well-known trademarks. He held that we have no choice but to consider things in terms of some background perspective within which we are, in effect, always already immersed, regardless of whether this perspective is that of the human being, of one's time period, of one's culture, of oneself as an individual, or the more grand perspective of life itself, within which we participate as breathing, down-to-earth, and perishable beings. A "perspectiveless perspective" or a view "from nowhere in particular and from everywhere at once," Nietzsche regarded as practically impossible and as thoroughly unrealistic.

The historical inspiration for Nietzsche's perspectivism is Immanuel Kant, whose philosophy was dedicated to articulating one very characteristic, finite perspective, namely, the human perspective. Kant claimed, almost as a matter of obvious definition, that human beings can know things only within the framework of the human perspective, and that outside the manageable and managing constraints of this human perspective, we can prove nothing at all. The saving grace of Kant's view, as far as Kant himself believed, is that because we are all human beings, we must all interpret things in exactly the same human way. Our limited human standpoint remains a shared one – one which coordinates our individual interpretations with each other from the very start. Human nature might stand in the way of ultimate knowledge, but it keeps our community intact and in interpretive harmony. For Kant, we may be barred forever from entering the garden of absolute knowledge, but we can rest with the philosophical certainty that we think in concert.

Kant spoke rigidly about the structure of the human perspective, having defined it in an abstracted way independently of individual differences, and indeed, independently of all the changing historical details of human experience. He conceived of "human nature" as a timeless abstraction, whose nature can be discerned by means of purely reflective thought. Having set historical differences aside, he identified and specified a single perspective that all humans allegedly share, going so far as to say that space and time, geometry and mathematics, were themselves constituents of this human perspective, and that if there were no humans, then space, time, and the laws of nature could very well amount to nothing at all.

Much of Nietzsche's thought is Schopenhauerian, and since Schopenhauer himself was a Kantian, we find markedly Kantian dimensions within Nietzsche's perspective. But just as Schopenhauer modified some of Kant's insights, Nietzsche developed Kant's views in his own unique way. Temperamentally, Nietzsche was less speculative, more pragmatic, and in a broad sense, more scientific, and he interpreted the foundation of the human condition, not in reference to a single perspective understood in terms of pure thought-categories, as did Kant, but in reference to more experience-centered categories, such as "life," "physiology," "biology," "environment," "climate," "strength," and "diet," to name a few. Among these, the concept of "life" was central from the start. One could almost say that Nietzsche's philosophy expresses the perspective of life – one which, although it stands as only one among many theoretical possibilities, remains a practically unavoidable perspective for anyone alive. It follows, by definition, that a living being must adopt the perspective of life if it intends to live very long.

In "On Truth and Lie in a Morally-Disengaged Sense," Nietzsche thought seriously about how concepts such as "truth" and "falsity" appear through the "perspective of life." Ordinarily, and notably from a moral perspective, lies are typically regarded as negatively valued and truths are typically regarded as positively valued. From the perspective of life, things look different, and the valuations change. Nietzsche observed that weaker and less robust people often preserve themselves, or maintain their life, by lying, cheating, flattering, deceiving, camouflaging, and by other such means of deception. For the purposes of survival, maintaining false appearances can be extremely useful, which is to say that from the perspective of life, lying and cheating are not entirely objectionable and inappropriate, if one happens to be a weaker type. If one were extremely weak and desperate, it might even be that one could lose one's life or one's livelihood, if one did not constantly lie and cheat. The perspective of life is not a fundamentally moral perspective. When it comes to basic survival, morality loses its relevance when an individual's sheer will-to-live raises its self-preserving head. For Nietzsche, this is a fact of life.

When interpreting matters from the perspective of life, it is necessary to consider not only matters of survival, reproduction, health, and overall quality of life – all of which Nietzsche discusses at one point or another – but the ways in which survival, health, etc., are maintained by individuals of various kinds. Since people, and life forms in general, differ in their respective strengths and capacities, different strategies for living distinguish themselves. It is this more discriminating attitude that separates Nietzsche from Kant. Whereas Kant rested content to articulate a single, universalized, human perspective, Nietzsche looked carefully at the specifics that govern people's perspectives, case by case, group by group, and among these he considered differences in physiology, environmental conditions, and temperamental conditions, and he developed typologies of the stronger and weaker types, utilizing these discriminations to analyze all sorts of cultural phenomena. For this reason, there is much talk about different religious, ethnic, and national groups scattered throughout Nietzsche's writings, where he compares and contrasts these groups in reference to their various survival styles. In this vein, and much later in his career, Nietzsche expressed the need to consider as well all moral imperatives as the linguistic embodiments of varying physiological conditions – conditions which he considered to be more basic than conscious states of mind:

> In fact all tables of values – all "you ought to's" – which we know from history or ethnological research, in any case, first require a *physiological* examination and interpretive explication, before even a psychological one; similarly, all of them stand in need of a critique from the side of medical science.[46]

In his early essay on truth and lies, we find Nietzsche at the outset of his project of understanding the world through the perspective of life. His view at this point is that what is commonly accepted as "the truth" is mostly a construction, mostly something artificial and fictional, that has nonetheless become stabilized in people's minds for the purposes of community survival. Commonly accepted "truths" amount to sets of social constructions that have become solidified in the language we use, and which appear to the population at large as being natural and true, precisely to the degree that they remain stable and unquestionably accepted.

From the days of the ancient Greeks, if not earlier, what is "true" has been considered to be what is stable, unchanging, and reliable, and Nietzsche appears to have accepted this view through most of his career. What he observed under the influence of Kant and Schopenhauer, though, is that there are two levels of stability – the level of the genuine truth, which might remain largely unknowable, and the level of the constructed "truths" which people arrange for themselves as the stabilities or law-like structures by which they agree to live. Strictly speaking, these latter truths are not necessarily truths at all, but are mostly illusions which people use to live effectively. This is one of the key thoughts in this relatively early essay, and what remains ambivalent is Nietzsche's attitude towards such illusions, or falsities: sometimes he diminished their importance because they do not significantly represent the truth of things as they are in themselves; sometimes he elevated their importance because he was frequently far more interested in health and life than in truth, and in these contexts, he clearly preferred enlivening falsehoods to crushing truths.

Despite his interest in the perspective of life, and the requirements of healthy living, Nietzsche often expressed a strong desire to discern the genuine (rather than the artificial, perspective-of-life generated) truth, as unbearable as it might be, and he tended to deprecate the liars and self-deceivers of the world as weaklings, calling for all of us to "be honest with ourselves" in the face of the illusions we inherit. At one point, he called for the dissolution of *all* anthropomorphic projections, believing that these obscure the genuine truth, which he was convinced has nothing at all to do with human interests and human qualities. In light of this, we can read the following remark as expressing the idea that what is commonly called "truth" really amounts to myth or illusion – an illusion created by the poetic mind in the quest for life:

> What, then, is truth? A maneuverable army of metaphors, metonymies, anthropomorphisms – in short, a summation of human relationships which have been poetically and rhetorically heightened, transposed, and embellished, and which, after long use by a people, are considered to be solid, canonical, and binding: truths are illusions whose true nature has been forgotten.[47]

Nietzsche asserts here as true the proposition that "truths" are mostly illusions, and he operates philosophically with a distinction between the "genuine truth," as opposed to what is usually taken to be the truth, most of which he considered to be fiction.[48] This is to say that in Nietzsche's eyes, almost everyone lives in a waking dream; almost everyone lives with a strong dimension of the Apollonian, as opposed to the Dionysian, aspect of existence, where Apollonian beauty and sanity – in the sense of "sanitized" – rule throughout the day. To see the world in terms of the Dionysian aspect, the life aspect, the feral aspect is to apprehend that we live mostly in illusion, in a condition of being captivated by a mostly fantastic world a good portion of the time, where the tendency is to rest content with merely comforting shadows as if they were realities, and where reality is perceived as clothed, rather than as naked. To see the world in terms of the Dionysian aspect is also, by implication, to align oneself with the fountain of life-energies from which such poetic dress-ups and cover-ups emerge.

Nietzsche fundamentally agreed with Kant's pivotal statement that "the things which we intuit are not in themselves what we intuit them as being."[49] Whether there are things in themselves that can be known, or whether there are indeed any "things" at all at the level of reality as it is in itself are yet further questions. At this point in his career – and this would be a view that would stay with Nietzsche at least up until 1886 – he recognized that there is an "illusion" or "appearance," which implies that there is an underlying "reality" to which one implicitly refers. In his final two years, as we shall see in Chapter Five, Nietzsche aimed to dissolve this distinction between "appearance" and "reality" alto-gether, leaving us to speak only of the single world of experience and existence.

3

God's death

Spiritual crisis and the healthful Greeks long lost

By the late 1700s, the Industrial Revolution was beginning to reveal its ambivalent effects in Europe. The development of manufacturing and the increased availability of material goods no doubt had its economic benefits, but this was had at a heavy human price. For the previous 150 years or so, the prevailing intellectual spirit had imagined the universe to be a large mechanism, and it was becoming evident that the development of manufacturing was reinforcing a cultural condition where human beings themselves were being pressed into mechanical labor as parts of factory-like social machines. This trend preoccupied Karl Marx (1818–83) during the later 1800s, and it was brought into literary expression earlier in the nineteenth century by Charles Dickens (1812–70), but as early as 1794, Friedrich Schiller (1759–1805) expressed his worries about the social conditions that were becoming typical of the "modern" age – conditions that were mentally fragmenting the human being, undermining spiritual harmony, and threatening to narrow down people's labor to circumscribed and superficial activities.[50] In the Sixth Letter of his *Letters on the Aesthetic Education of Humanity* (1794), Schiller observed the following:

As soon as more wide-ranging experience and more exact modes of thought required a sharper division of the sciences on the one hand, and on the other, as the complicated clockwork of States required a stronger separation of the social classes and occupations, so was the inner bond of human nature also divided, and a corrupting conflict set its harmonious powers against each other. Intuitive and speculative understanding set themselves off from each other antagonistically upon their respective fields, whose borders they now began to guard with distrust and jealousy, and in this narrowing-down of our activity to a single sphere, we have also given ourselves up to a single ruler, who, frequently enough, is disposed to repress the remaining capacities. Whereas on one occasion an extravagant imagination ravages the hard-won fruits of the intellect, the spirit of abstract thought crushes the fire that might have warmed the heart and inspired imaginative fancy.[51]

Schiller's observations foreshadowed those of Karl Marx, written in 1848 at the age of thirty, and published fifty-four years later:

Modern industry has transformed the small workspace of the patriarchal master-craftsmen into the large factories of industrial capitalism. Masses of workers, pressed together in the factories, have been organized like soldiers. They are like common industry-soldiers set up under the complete hierarchy of officers and subordinates. They are not only servants of the bourgeoisie, of the bourgeois-state, they are daily and hourly made to be servants of the machine, of the overseers, and above all, of the single bourgeois manufacturer itself. This despotism is even more petty, hateful, and embittering, the more it proclaims "acquisition" to be its goal.[52]

The situation had not become so dire when Schiller was writing in the late 1700s, and he retained a strong faith that the human condition could be healed, believing that people could be spiritually rejuvenated, if only they had a healthier outlook towards which to turn. As a remedy, Schiller recalled the classical Greeks for inspiration, because the Christian Church at the time – at least in many people's eyes – had become too ritualized, worldly, and detached from the spiritual problems that had arisen as a side-effect of the overly mechanical and deterministic vision of the world that had transformed it into a giant clockwork. Since institutionalized Christianity was not providing the inspiration that was expected, many turned elsewhere for spiritual nourishment, either in an effort to reform the prevailing Church, or in an effort to import an entirely new religious inspiration from elsewhere. A good many intellectuals turned to the classical Greeks for inspiration; among them was Schiller, who was convinced that "the phenomenon of Greek humanity was indisputably a maximum which could neither be maintained at that level nor be surpassed."[53]

Calling the ancient Greeks to the rescue, however, was not an easy matter. Schiller, along with others who hoped for a reinstitution of the Greek spirit, soon realized that the Greek culture no longer existed in the form it had during the time of classical Greece, and that it was, in fact, long gone. The Greek sculptures were no longer infused with the spirits of the gods, as the gods had once stood there, glowing and radiating from the sculpted stone figures. These artworks were no longer perceivable as they had been thousands of years ago; they had turned to stone, and their animating spirits had flown. Greek art was long dead. So although there was, on the one hand, the hope of reinstituting the Greek spirit, there was an accompanying emptiness in the awareness that the classical Greek times were not the present times. The idea of being a "modern" person who sought to become an "ancient" person generated theoretical problems that emerged throughout the literature of the period.[54] Frequently enough, what one finds during this late eighteenth and early nineteenth century period is an uncertainty about how to express exactly what was sought from the classical Greeks. It was admitted that the Greek gods were no longer culturally alive, but there was a confidence that the Greek spirit could somehow be incorporated into European culture, even though this new life had to be in some contemporary, or future, form.[55]

This cultural situation soon generated a sense of disillusionment: the Christianity of the time was perceived to be spiritually dying, and the rejuvenation to be attained by a return to the Greek spirit became undermined by the growing realization that the Greek gods had already turned into stone. The increasingly frequent use of the phrase "God is dead" in philosophic and literary expression is evidence of the growing spiritual crisis.

Nietzsche himself used the phrase "God is dead" for the first time explicitly in 1882 (in *The Gay Science*, §108), but this phrase occurs within philosophical texts as early as 1804 and 1807.[56] In these earlier instances, the phrase is used to refer either to the crucifixion (where Jesus-as-God dies), or to the spiritual crisis of the devout believer, who has sacrificed everything for God, only to discover that this sacrifice has not borne any spiritual fruit or any "response" from God. After having sacrificed everything to God, and then having later found no definite presence of God, devout believers would often fall into a condition where there was nothing left in which to believe – a condition, in effect, of utter nihilism. This is a spiritual condition comparable to that of the disillusioned believer in God, who asks how God can allow crimes against humanity to happen, and allow them to go unpunished.

In his *Phenomenology of Spirit* (1807), Hegel offers a memorable characterization of this dark night of the soul, having in mind the experience of the disillusioned devotee.[57] For Hegel, the perception of God's death – especially as it is experienced by a formerly devout believer – leads dreadfully to absolute disillusionment. Here, the loss of faith in God is understood in a general and philosophical sense, namely, as the loss of acknowledgment of stable, universal realities. Hegel believes that the former devotee, now having nothing more upon which to rely, sinks into an exclusive, one-sided focus upon individual concerns. And insofar as the disillusioned individual becomes preoccupied with merely individual matters, he or she observes that the person is reduced to pettiness, self-centeredness, and utter finitude. This specific understanding of this spiritual debilitation recognizes most importantly that at the center of the nihilistic consciousness is a sense of loss, emptiness, solitude, and despair. Nihilistic conscious-ness issues when the ground of one's spiritual substance is removed, and one falls into the belief that there is nothing of permanent meaning for which to live.[58]

Nihilism and the "death of God"

To sense the emotional depth that is likely to have motivated Nietzsche's discussions of the death of God, we can reflect on the kinds of emotions that accompany the death of anyone whom one has depended on and loved. The general psychology of the situation is well documented. First, there is an initial experience of shock and disbelief, followed by profound emotional pain and a growing sense of emptiness. Then, the pain slowly subsides and the emptiness gradually becomes replaced with more satisfying meaning as one readjusts and reconstitutes one's outlook in a constructive way, once one has, ideally, grown to accept the loved person's non-presence. Typically involved in the experience is a severe loss of personal significance, a disorientation that results from the disruption, if not complete disintegration, of what had been a primary source of spiritual nourishment, not to mention a sense of fear as a consequence of having been left relatively alone by the person's death. Recovery from such a loss is not a necessary result; cases of spouses dying immediately after the death of their husband or wife are known, and cases of individuals who slowly die of heartbreak after the death of their loved ones are familiar.

Whether Nietzsche was ever a completely devout and commit-ted Christian during any time in his life is an open question, but it is undeniable that his father was a minister, that his early years were centered around his father's church and accompanying pastor's house (located only meters away from the church), and that the kind of music he wrote in his teens is clearly in the style of church music. That his father – who Nietzsche loved – died when he was only four years old, followed by his younger, two-year-old brother only six months later, can be added here as additional facts of significance. Nietzsche's early childhood experiences presented him with an understanding of death that could easily be transposed into reflections on the "death of God," if only because the Christian God is a superhuman father-figure.[59]

Despite the available biographical evidence which can ground some speculations, it is impossible to know what the full psychological impact the death of Nietzsche's father and younger brother was. We are on more stable ground, if, to understand the idea of the "death of God," we consider what it would mean to add the word "absolute" before the kinds of experiences, mentioned above, that are typically involved in the loss of a loved one. Rather than experiencing a "severe" loss of personal meaning – one that is devastating enough literally to kill some people – one would experience an "absolute" loss of personal meaning and consequently suffer from feelings of utter emptiness. Rather than experiencing a disorientation resulting from the disruption of one's personal meaning, one would experience an "absolute disorientation," a complete groundlessness, or an abysmal absurdity. Rather than experiencing fear, one would experience absolute terror. Rather than feeling lonely, one would feel absolutely alone and completely abandoned.

Given the extremes of emotion involved here, it is easy to see how the "death of God," if experienced by a person of previously deep faith in God, could lead to an attitude of nihilism and psychological destitution. The deeper one's belief in God, the more maddening, and more life-threatening, God's death would be. In principle, the "death of God" is an extremely dangerous idea which has the power to dynamite one's sense of integrated personal meaning. For some people, retaining the belief in God could be a matter of survival.

During Nietzsche's lifetime, nihilistic attitudes were becoming noticeable within European culture. As noted, Christianity was perceived by many to be in a spiritual crisis, and some of the hopes that alternative efforts for rejuvenation – such as a return to the classical Greeks – were proving to be ineffective. Within this context, we can understand how Nietzsche might have been motivated to discover a new source of cultural strength. What is particular about his approach is that he judged that the "death" of God was not the core problem: the more fundamental reason for the spiritual crisis in the Christian culture that surrounded him, he believed, was that positive belief in the Christian God was itself debilitating. Nietzsche judged that the Christian culture was in an unhealthy condition, not because it had lost its inspirational cornerstone, but because the foundations of its inspiration were themselves unsound. The belief in the "life" of God appeared to be more spiritually impairing than the belief in the "death" of God. Nietzsche concluded that a fundamental tenet of Christianity – the belief in a supernatural, all-knowing, all-powerful, all-good God – was itself unhealthy, mainly because it distracted people from the world here-and-now.[60] It is one thing to be devastated by the death of one's spouse; it is quite another to realize that prior to that death, one's relationship to the loved one had been altogether diseased.

Nietzsche as physician for modern Europe

If we pursue, in a social-psychological way, an interpretation of the nihilistic attitude Nietzsche discerned within his culture –

namely, as a reaction of grief to the "death of God" – we can perceive Nietzsche as someone who, when addressing his culture, was speaking to a group of people who were already in the midst of suffering a major loss, or who were on the verge of realizing this loss explicitly. This would be the population of those who still "believed in God," but who felt that there probably was no God. It would also include the population of those who had decided that there was no God, and who had not yet arrived at a constructive way of adapting to the situation. The former group – those who perceived God to be dying – would include those who continued to attend church services in a ritualistic way, who continued to give superficial acknowledgment to prevailing religious rules and beliefs, and who continued to "go through the motions" of being Christians, while at the same time feeling hopeless. The latter group – those who perceived God to be dead – would include those people who gave up on Christianity and believed in nothing at all.

Once Nietzsche became convinced that the very belief in God was unhealthy, his own vantage point became comparable to that of a physician who intends to treat a patient with a life-threatening disease. If the disease is still at a latent stage, the patient might not acknowledge the serious character of the disease; if the disease is at a manifest stage, the person might give up hope, and refuse treatment altogether. The physician, faced with such extremes, might still proceed diligently to work on administering a cure, or developing a therapy. In connection with the "social disease" Nietzsche perceived within his European culture, we can understand him as first having diagnosed the disease, then having made an effort to communicate the disease to those who refused to listen, and, in spite of this frustration, having devoted himself to developing a constructive outlook which could serve as a cure and a means to the restoration of social health.

Specifically, Nietzsche's diagnosis was that the belief in the Christian God was making people spiritually depressed, in a large part due to the guilt-generating scrutiny of people's souls that such an all-powerful seer exerted. Nietzsche's initial prescription to the spiritually depressed was, therefore, that this other-worldly God must be "killed," if health and self-confidence were to be restored. This God had to be eliminated, moreover, in such a way that people could experience the grief process, and live through the nihilistic outlook in full force. He believed that only after the previously existing spiritual and emotional dependence on the Christian God had been put behind would everyone – or at least those strong enough to endure this exorcistic and purgatorial process – be in the position to adopt life-affirming interpretations of the world that would remain with them. Most, if not all, of the main themes within Nietzsche's philosophy can be located within this "Nietzsche-as-physician/Nietzsche-as-funeral minister/Nietzsche-as-psychiatrist" framework.

In the Vedic medicine of traditional India, it was customary first to make a diagnosis of the person's disease. Next, the cause of the disease was determined. Then the decision was made whether or not the disease was fatal. Finally, a therapy was prescribed, if the patient was believed to be curable. Most famously, Buddha's fourfold truths follow this structure: life is suffering; the cause of suffering is desire; there is a way to control one's desire; a certain path of belief and activity can be specified to achieve this end. Nietzsche's philosophy is organized in the same way, except that he identifies a different disease, and prescribes a different cure. In the end, both accept the phrase, "Overcome your greatest desire, and you will become enlightened." In Buddhism, one overcomes one's greatest desire for the sake of overcoming desire itself. In Nietzscheanism, one overcomes one's greatest desire for the sake of experiencing an even more profound and healthy desire.

The diagnosis: theism is a spiritual debilitation

As we have seen, Nietzsche believed that one major reason why the people in his Christian culture were spiritually unhealthy was because their faith in the Christian God had made them unhealthy. He was not dead-set against all conceptions of the divine; he aimed his barbs quite specifically at one particular conception:

> The Christian conception of God ... is one of the most corrupt conceptions of God that has ever been attained on this planet; it represents, perhaps, the low-water-mark in the descending development of divine types. God devolved into the *contradiction of life*, instead of its transfiguration and eternal *Yes*! God as the expression of hostility against life, against nature, against the will to life. God as the formula for every slander against "this life," for every lie about "the next life"! God as nothingness turned into a god, the will to nothingness pronounced holy![61]

Nietzsche maintained that the conception of the Christian God inverts healthy interpretations of the world, insofar as it draws our attention away from the daily world. God, as defined within the Christian conception Nietzsche had in mind, is fundamentally a spaceless and timeless being, and to the extent that our interests and personal meanings remain centered in the timeless, otherworldly realm of God, our lives are not grounded in the daily world of space and in time – the realm where we must live our flesh-and-blood lives. Nietzsche believed that the dominant conception of the Christian God is life-negating, or world-negating, and that it amounts to a "deification of nothingness," for it diverts our attention from the world we live in, and hence, disengages us from life itself.

According to Nietzsche, the Christian conception of God is not only life-negating in the indirect sense that it distracts us from the daily world; the very actions of this God are directly life-negating.

Since the Christian God is conceived to be an absolute moral judge – one who condemns people for expressing their purely animal urges – and since a significant aspect of these animal urges involves the instinct to reproduce the species, it would seem that the Christian conception of God significantly constricts the expression of sexual energies.[62] In Nietzsche's view, this restriction is enforced by the imposition of overwhelming guilt – a guilt that he believes is so extensive and so foundational that it becomes impossible to live in a condition where one is not guilty.

As far as Nietzsche can see, this theistic outlook amounts to a form of madness, and he reasons that the kind of sickness with which he sees the European Christian as having been infected is a mental illness. He regards the Christian conception of God as one that drives people insane, partly because living according to this conception has the deranging effect of suppressing instinctual energies whose expression is a condition for an organism's health and mental balance: [63]

A guilt before *God*: this thought becomes an instrument of torture to him. He apprehends in "God" the ultimate opposition to his own inextinguishable animal-instincts; he regards these animal-instincts themselves as a kind of guilt before God (as hostility, revolt, uprising against the "Master," the "Father," the primal forefather and source of the world); he extends and suspends himself upon the contradiction between "God" and "Devil"; he denies that which his own being says of himself – nature, naturalness, actuality – in order to erect out of it a "yes"; a "yes" as existent, bodily, real, as God, as the holiness of God, as God-the-Judge, as God-the-hangman, as the beyond, as eternity, as endless torture, as hell, as the immeasurability of punishment and guilt.

This is a kind of madness of the will which, in its spiritual cruelty, is absolutely unparalleled: the will to find oneself guilty and reprehensible to the point of unatonability; a *will* to consider oneself punished such that the punishment could never be equal to the guilt; a *will* to infect and poison the deepest ground of things with the problem of punishment and guilt, in order to cut off completely, an exit from this labyrinth of "fixed ideas"; a will to erect an ideal – that of the "holy God" – and in light of this ideal to be certain, first-hand, of one's absolute unworthiness. The human being: what an insane and pathetic beast! What notions come to mind, what perversities, what attacks of madness, what *bestiality of thought* comes forth, when a person is only hindered a bit, from being a *beast in action*!

This is interesting to the point of excess, but it is also of a dark, dismal, and unnerving sadness, such that one must forcibly forbid oneself to look too long into these bottomless pits. Here is *sickness*, without a doubt – the most awful sickness which has raged in the human being to date; and whoever is still able to hear (but there are no longer any ears for this!), how, in this night of torment and madness, the cry of *love*, the cry of the most ardent delight, the redemption in *love*, will turn themselves away, seized by an unconquerable, skin-crawling horror. There is so much in people that is appalling! The earth has been a madhouse for too long![64]

Nietzsche's reaction to the condition of the Christian culture, stated above at the end of his career, echoes Schopenhauer's adverse reaction to the qualities he perceived in the human condition in general. With Nietzsche, the sad state of affairs does not always extend to every nook and cranny within the human being as a whole, and he allows some room for hope. But one thing is clear: he perceives that the human society surrounding him is in a diseased spiritual state, and that something needs to be done, lest the entire species waste away. He takes it upon himself to spread the word that there is a prevailing sickness in society, held by the conviction that even if people do not realize that they are spiritually ill at present, the time will come when they will realize it in full force.

Part of the sickness which Nietzsche associates with belief in God involves the sense of overwhelming guilt that such a belief generates. In *Thus Spoke Zarathustra*, one of Nietzsche's literary characters – the "ugliest man," who is the murderer of God – accordingly explains his motives. As a prelude to the further excerpts where Nietzsche introduces the theme of the "death of God," it is useful to reflect upon some of the motivations surrounding not the mere "death," but the "murder" of God:

> "But he … *had* to die: he saw with eyes that saw everything – he saw the depths and grounds of people; he saw all of their hidden humiliation and ugliness. His pity had no shame: he creeped into my dirtiest corners. This absolutely-curious, too-intrusive, too-pitying one had to die. He *always* saw me: I wanted to have revenge on such a witness – or else not live. The God who saw everything, *everyone included* – this God had to die! A person cannot stand it, that such a witness should live."

> Thus spoke the ugliest person. But then Zarathustra got up and prepared himself to leave, for his blood had run cold …

> Thus spoke Zarathustra, and he went his way, more pensively and slowly than before: for he asked himself much and had no easy answers.

> "Everyone is really so poor!" he thought in his heart, "how ugly, how groaning, how filled with hidden shame! I was once told that people love themselves: ah, how great must this self-love be! It has so much contempt against it! This man also loved himself, just as he despised himself – he is a great lover to me, and also a great despiser. I haven't found anyone who has hated himself more than him: and *that* is also something great. Perhaps *he* was the higher person whose cry I heard? I love the great despisers. The human being, though, is something that has to be overcome."[65]

The idea of experiencing desire and guilt in connection with the "murder" of a father-figure becomes, in later years, a central proposition – the Oedipus Complex – in Sigmund Freud's psychoanalytic theory, and this guilt-related theme adds another dimension to Nietzsche's "death of God" discussion.[66] For Freud, the wish to murder one's father (or, if one is a woman, the wish to murder one's mother), is consistent with the drive for personal autonomy.[67] Once one is free from the dominating forces of one's parents, one is free to create one's own values and to regard oneself as a unique person. The "murder of God" in the above passage is intended to have similar effects, but at a more expanded level of cultural consciousness: without God – so it is thought – there is no single, true interpretation of the world; without God, there is no single, true set of moral values; without God, there is no supreme judge who determines one's ultimate reward and/or punishment; without God, reality itself no longer can make one feel guilty and psychologically stressed from over-surveillance, as if one were living in a cosmic penitentiary with an all-powerful jailer. The drive for individuality and freedom motivates the "death of God" theme in Nietzsche, which is to say that Nietzsche considers himself to be a champion of freedom, not to mention an absolute lawbreaker, styling himself as akin to Satan.

There is, uncomfortably, at least one paradoxical dimension of Nietzsche's discussion of guilt in reaction to God's "murder." It is strange that the "ugliest man" – the "murderer of God" – suffers guilt for having killed God. If "God" represents the source of Christian morality, and if this being is rendered impotent, then the result should be that guilt is eliminated. Rather than feeling infinitely guilty for having killed God, the ugliest man should feel no guilt at all, since the elimination of guilt is among the purposes of killing God. The situation, then, as Nietzsche presents it, involves a dilemma: when God exists, one feels guilty because God condemns one morally; when one "kills" God, one feels guilty for having killed a supreme being.

A more consistent way to understand the matter would be to say that once one "kills" God, one has reached a standpoint beyond good and evil, and will no longer experience any guilt. The "murder of God" leads ideally to a guilt-free, non-moral standpoint. Nietzsche's "ugliest man" still lives in the "shadows" of God, and has not stepped into what Nietzsche believes to be the guilt-free, more beautiful and healthy daylight, which is to say that Nietzsche's staunch advocacy of atheism probably troubled him at times, for he saw himself as one of God's chief murderers.

Breaking the news: communicating to a senseless patient

Insofar as Nietzsche felt frustrated in his attempts to communicate to his intended audience that belief in God makes people unhealthy, his position is similar to that of psychiatrists who often face a comparably frustrating situation when they try to explain to a patient that there is something the matter with him or her, but have difficulty reaching any acknowledgment of this fact by the patient, because the patient's own mental condition prevents him or her from absorbing the message. Indeed, when such a clash of perspective arises it is sometimes difficult to determine which party, if either, has the more reality-based perspective. [68]

In Nietzsche's own writings, we find this same kind of communicational impasse arising when he (in the guise of one of his literary characters) tries to express the idea that "God is dead." Perhaps the most important of these passages is one from *The Gay Science* (1882) entitled "The Crazy One," in which an apparently crazy man tries to inform a group of villagers about God's death, only to be met with mocking laughter. Those to whom the madman speaks appear on the face of things to be disbelievers in God, because their reactive comments to him do not respect the idea of God. These people can be understood to include among them those members of the Christian society to which Nietzsche belongs, who accept traditional moral values, but who are not especially religious or devout in their beliefs. Neither group – the set of insensitive disbelievers who do not reflect on the full meaning of "God's death," and the set of insensitive believers who do not reflect on the full meaning of "God's existence" – thinks very deeply about the significance of what they supposedly disbelieve or believe.

Nietzsche is addressing the group of superficial people who simply follow the existing traditional views, who let these views unconsciously regulate their lives, and who end up becoming the victims of those unconsidered outlooks. Rather than imagining the group to be one of reflective souls, it is closer to "the mob" which does not often behave in a sophisticated manner, and whose views on religious matters are often not clearly considered. It is fair to say that Nietzsche regarded all such people as "Christian" insofar as they adopted the prevailing ways and values of the Christian culture at large. For him, they were asleep, and he could not easily wake them up.

All in all, the situation is perspectivally complicated: those who devoutly believe in God are driven mad by God's death; those who are insensitive to God in general, alive or dead, are mad insofar as they cannot feel the spiritual problem; those who strongly believe that God is dead and who have come to terms with this appear to be mad to those who do not possess this belief. There is madness all around, from one perspective to another. Or alternatively described, there is a set of disjointed perspectives standing side-by-side in a single, uneasy community.

When Nietzsche asserts in the following passage that "we" have all killed God, he is trying to draw attention to a general lack of awareness within the prevailing culture: it is a "Christian" culture, and yet it is without spiritual depth. So there is a double problem. Everyone around Nietzsche tended to accept the traditional moral values that are linked with belief in God, and yet not many people were thinking searchingly about what it means to be either a Christian or an atheist. Nietzsche, consequently, had an argument with devout Christians of spiritual depth and reflection, but also an argument with merely nominal Christians who embody superficiality, or shallowness, in their religious thinking.

The following expresses almost all of the themes surrounding the "death of God" – disillusionment, madness, guilt, disorientation – that appear in many of Nietzsche's later passages on the same theme:

> *The crazy one.* – Have you not heard of the crazy one, who lit a lantern in the middle of the bright morning, ran to the market place and continually shouted out: "I am looking for God! I am looking for God!" There were many standing around who did not believe in God, so he aroused a great deal of laughter. Has he somehow gotten lost? one said. Has he run away, like a child? said another. Or is he hiding? Is he afraid of us? Has he taken a ship? Left the country? – so they laughed and cried out in a group.
>
> The crazy one jumped into the middle of them and bored into them with his gaze. "Where is God?," he cried, "I will tell you! *We have killed him* – you and I! We are all his murderers. But how have we done this? How were we able to drink up the sea? Who gave us the sponge to wipe away the whole horizon? What did we do when we unchained this earth from its sun? Where is it moving now? Where are we moving? Away from all suns? Are we not constantly falling? And going backwards, sideways, forwards, in all directions? Is there still an "above" and "below"? Are we not wandering as through an endless nothingness? Doesn't the emptiness of space breathe at us? It has become colder, has it not? Is not night, and more night, continually coming at us? Should not lanterns then be lit in the morning? Do we not yet hear the sound of the gravediggers who are burying God? Do we not yet smell the divine decay – divinities also decay! God is dead! God remains dead! And we have killed him!
>
> How can we console ourselves, we murderers of all murderers? The most holy and powerful that the world has ever seen, has bled to death by our knives – and who is going to wipe the blood from

our hands? With what water can we cleanse ourselves? What atonement-festivals, what holy games do we need to create? Is not the immensity of this deed too immense for us? Do we not have to become gods ourselves, in order to appear to be worthy of it? There has never been a greater deed – and whoever comes after us, thus belongs to this deed, and to a higher history than ever before!"

At this point the crazy one became silent, and he looked at his audience: they also became silent and looked at him, completely taken aback. Finally, he threw his lantern to the ground, where it broke into pieces and went out. "I am here too soon," he then said, "It is not yet my proper time. This monstrous event is still under-way and wandering – it has still not penetrated people's ears. Lightning and thunder need time, the light of the stars needs time, deeds need time to be seen and heard, even though they are already done. To them, this deed is further away than the farthest star – *and yet they have done it themselves!*"

It was further said, that the crazy one broke into a number of churches on the same day, and chanted his *Requiem aeternam deo.*[69] Led away and called to explain himself, he always said the same thing: "What are these churches, then, if not the crypts and tombs of God." [70]

In *Thus Spoke Zarathustra*, Nietzsche expressed the same frustration in his efforts to communicate the ideas that "God is dead" and that one must love the earth instead. The following section – in which Zarathustra takes the literary place of "the crazy one" – is parallel in spirit to the one above:

But Zarathustra became sad and said to his heart: "They do not understand me: I am not the mouth for these ears. Too long have I lived in the mountains, too long have I listened to the streams and to the trees: now I talk to them as to goatherds. My soul is steadfast and bright like the mountains in the morning. But they think I am cold, and that I despise them in terrible jest. And now they look at me and laugh: and while they laugh, they hate me still. In their laughter, there is ice.[71]

Nietzsche's rejuvenating injections

In light of the frustrations in communication Nietzsche expressed, he presented himself in writing as a doctor who discovers an as yet unperceived epidemic, who attempts to inform society at large, and who is confronted only with disbelief, denial, and mockery. Confident, however, in his diagnosis, the outcast doctor proceeds to develop a cure, knowing that the disease will manifest itself and that his medical assistance will be sought. Suspecting that the disease is going to become manifest only after he dies, he commits to writing the prescriptions for a cure to be used by future generations. At the end of his career, Nietzsche wrote:

> I am one thing, my writings are another thing. – Let me touch upon the question of their being understood or *not* understood, before I talk about each specifically. I will do it as informally as is appropriate, because this question is really not yet timely. I, myself, am not yet timely; some are born posthumously.
>
> People will someday need institutions, in which one lives and teaches in the way I understand living and teaching: it might even be, that there will be some teaching positions established for the interpretation of *Zarathustra*. But it would be a perfect contradiction to my nature, if I already expected ears *and hands* for *my* truths: that people today do not hear, that people pick up nothing from me, is not only understandable, it even appears to me to be proper.[72]

> I am a Gospel like no other; I know tasks of such a height, that there has not been any concept of them to date; beginning with me, are there again hopes.[73]

> I am by far the most awful person that has ever been up until now; that does not rule out that I will be the most beneficent.[74]

Nietzsche perceived that the society around him was operating in accord with a religious outlook that was draining everyone's vitality. In response to this life-negating condition, he developed a remedy: an array of alternative interpretations of the world that he considered to be less guilt-generating and more life-affirming, because they were completely down to earth. These alternative, anti-Christian, interpretations form the major components of Nietzsche's positive philosophical outlook, and they include some of his most well-known ideas such as the "will to power," the "superhuman" being, the judgment that life itself is "beyond good and evil," and the doctrine of "eternal recurrence." Located at the core of Nietzsche's thought is a concern with the overall health of humanity, as expressed in his concept of "life-affirmation" − a concept which he crystallized into various manifestations, depending on whether he was reflecting on the universe as a whole, life as a whole, human beings in general, or the individual person. Watching from the shadows of Nietzsche's thought is also the nihilistic fear that his message would never be heard, and that his "untimely" life would never find its proper contemporaries.

4

Dissolving the shadows of God

Truth as a paralyzing Medusa

When the phrase "God is dead" occurs for the first time in Nietzsche's writings (*The Gay Science*, §108), we find Nietzsche directing our attention to the "shadows of God" that still, and which he expects will continue to, linger in Western society, long after the concept of "God" has faded from people's minds:

> *New struggles.* – After Buddha was dead, his shadow still appeared in a cave for hundreds of years – a monstrous, bloodcurdling shadow. God is dead: but given how people are, it might be that there will be caves in which his shadow appears for another thousand years. And we – we must also conquer his shadow.[75]

What are these "shadows of God"? Since God is regarded as the absolute foundation of things, the shadows of God include concepts that purport to be the timeless, unchanging, thoroughly reliable structures of what is. These assume different forms, depending on the religion, philosophy, science, or general belief system under consideration, but they share the characteristic of being supposedly invariant and unshakable. Among such "shadows," Nietzsche includes philosophical ideas such as "eternally enduring substances," "matter," and "Platonic Forms." One can further include the laws of nature and definitions of human nature that set limits upon (and for some theorists, falsely imprison us within a definite formulation of) our human condition. An implication of eliminating the conception of an absolutely foundational God, then, is that all kinds of eternal constancies are brought into question for the sake of opening up more wide-ranging human possibilities.

Nietzsche also described the "shadows of God" in another way, assuming that the universe as a whole has no human-like qualities. His view is that "God" is a concept that derives from the projection and amplification of certain human interests related to "knowledge," "goodness," "power," "freedom," and "intelligence" (God is all-knowing, all-good, all-powerful, is creative and self-determining, and is a planner or designer). Nietzsche believes that "God" is therefore an embodiment of strictly human concerns and qualities. This idea was not Nietzsche's own; it was expressed by Ludwig Feuerbach (1804–72) and David Hume (1711–76), among others. Nietzsche observed that even Xenophanes (570–475 BC) asserted that if horses and oxen could paint, they would paint their gods as horses and oxen. Nietzsche applied the same point to humans. Humans are often said to be made in God's image; here, it is God who is said to be made in the image of the human being.

Since Nietzsche believed that most of the human being's conceptual constructions function primarily to serve the interests of the human being *per se*, he hesitated to advance theories of the cosmos that involve superimpositions of human qualities onto the universe as a whole. Like Xenophanes, he resisted anthropomorphic interpretations of the world, especially when they are used to reflect some absolute, definitive truth. Such anthropomorphic interpretations, upon becoming absolute and accepted as eternally true, become the "shadows of God" in the first sense described above. Nietzsche accentuated how self-centered human beings actually are, and how illusory some of their ideas can become:

The human being, the Thespian of the world. – ... Perhaps the ant in the forest imagines that it is the goal and purpose of the forest's existence, just as strongly as we, in our fantasy, take the final point of humanity to be the final point of the earth: indeed, we are being modest if we stop at that, and do not recognize at the funeral rites of the one-that-is-finished, a twilight of the gods and twilight of the world.[76]

Nietzsche was entertained by the fact that humans continue to locate themselves at the meaning-center of the universe, just as they once believed that the sun, planets, and stars all revolved around the earth. As questionable as this self-centered orientation towards the universe might be, though, it does not imply that humans do not partake in, and are not a respectable part of, the cosmos as a whole. Moreover, whether one can entirely distance oneself from all anthropomorphic ascriptions to the universe, and whether the very enterprise of making such ascriptions is illegitimate, are debatable proposals. Since human beings are themselves part of the universe, and grow out of it, it stands to reason that some aspects of the human being must also be qualities of the whole.

Nietzsche's belief that no distinctively human qualities can be legitimately projected on to the universe as a whole, then, reflects a worldview within which humans are not fundamentally at home in the universe from which they were formed. His view resonates with those versions of Christianity that recognize a strong division between the spirit and the flesh, and between mind and matter. Although he wanted to advance a view where people are realistically integrated into and are considered to be an intrinsic part of the world, Nietzsche did not want to attribute any anthropomorphic qualities to the world as it is in itself. This generated a tension within his view in terms of understanding the human being's place in the universe: people are to be integrated into the world, but the world into which they are to be integrated is regarded as an inhuman one. Nietzsche urged that people work to find themselves finally at home in the world, although the home in which they must dwell contains ineradicably alien aspects. The situation is comparable to someone who wants to love his or her parents unconditionally, even though they have been mentally dislocated by the fact that their parents have been mind-numbingly cruel if not criminal, at times, just as Mother Nature can be cruel and immoral.

Nietzsche thus intended to avoid anthropomorphizing the universe as much as is possible, and in light of this desire, he stated that the world is fundamentally a chaos, or a realm ruled by chance:

> The overall character of the world is, to the contrary, in all eternity chaos – not in the sense of any necessity that is missing, but an absence of order, structuring, form, beauty, wisdom, and everything else named by our aesthetic, human constructions.[77]

> Nature, considered artistically, is no model. It exaggerates, it distorts, it leaves holes. Nature is *chance*.[78]

> And it is not always purpose, that is referred to as such, and even less is everything will, that is called will! And, if you want to conclude: "There is therefore only one realm, that of accidents and stupidity?" – so one should add: yes, perhaps there is only one realm, perhaps there is neither will nor purposes, and we have only imagined it all. Those iron hands of necessity which shake the dice-box of chance, play their game forever: so some throws *must* come out of that, which appear to be similar, in each degree, to purposiveness and rationality.[79]

As opposed to a global environment ruled securely by rigid constancies and predictabilities – constancies that Nietzsche associated with the shadows of God and with stagnation – his interpretation of the world as a fiery chaos more effectively expresses a life-affirming outlook, owing to its consistency with change and creativity. Since some of the central characteristics Nietzsche associated with "life" are growth, creativity, change, metamorphosis, expansion, and destruction, the interpretation of the universe as continually flickering and fluctuating is more consistent with these values than is a completely rigid, deterministic, thoroughly rule-governed definition, where freedom and the development of new possibilities are set at a relative minimum, or set within a kind of conceptual cage. Since there is a perpetual uncertainty about what the nature of the universe happens to be, Nietzsche advocated that we adopt the interpretation that best serves the interests of life, whether or not it is provably true. He consequently celebrated change, instability, danger, destruction, and challenge, to match his accentuation of life and creativity.

Such an interpretation of the universe might present itself as far more joyously thrilling than frightening, given Nietzsche's emphasis on play, creativity, unpredictability, enticing and daring danger, growth, and dance. But there is a hard and icy side to this vision – one that can turn a soft, sentimental, and rationality-seeking person into stone, as can happen when a person looks squarely into an embittering moral abyss. For Nietzsche's vision recognizes no eternal justice at all. The criminals who get away with their crimes simply get away with their crimes. His universe is not concerned with such matters.

The nature of life: beyond good and evil

Nietzsche, at one point, referred to himself as an "experimental biologist," intending to express his interest in interpreting human experience through the perspective of life. This emphasis on the concept of life was a common feature of his era: at the end of the eighteenth century, the prevailing conception of the natural order as a giant clockwork became frustratingly uninspiring, and it was soon replaced in the early nineteenth century by models that were grounded on principles that were more fluid, open, and in accordance with the world of human beings than with the workings of inanimate matter. During the nineteenth century, many philosophers began to formulate views more in accordance with "life," "growth," "development," and "creativity," and

Nietzsche was among them, although his particular view of life can be seen as noticeably tough-minded.[80]

With an attitude somewhat more scrutinizing than his early nineteenth-century predecessors, Nietzsche realized that if one were to philosophize in accordance with the concept of life, then one must accept a hard fact: life appears to be impossible without some measure of pain and violence. A thoroughly peaceful and painless world, or a thoroughly heavenly world – one which was, in fact, the ideal of much socialist, utilitarian, and Christian thought of the time – he saw as contradicting the nature of life. In such a non-violent world, for instance, neither plants nor animals could be killed for food. In terms of general belief-systems, phrases such as "all for one and one for all," or the "'I' that is 'we' and the 'we' that is 'I'" reveal themselves to be unrealistic, life-denying, ideals. Strongly opposing such outlooks, Nietzsche asked that we "be honest with ourselves," and admit squarely that "life *is* something immoral."[81] Which is to say that insofar as we are alive and breathing, what we self-righteously call "immorality" is an unavoidable part of our own living fabric.[82] To condemn something as "immoral," is, at a certain level of abstraction, the same as condemning oneself as a living being. It seems that we are all perpetrators:[83]

> One must give some real thought to the foundations here, resisting all sentimental weakness: life itself is *essentially* appropriation, wounding, taking over what is alien and weaker, oppression, harshness, forcing of one's own forms upon other beings, annexation, and at least, at its mildest, exploitation – but why should one always use such words, which for the longest time have been stamped with a slanderous intent?[84]

> Life operates *essentially*, namely, in its basic functions, with injury, violation, exploitation, destruction, and cannot at all be conceived without this character. One must stand by an even further thought: that, from the highest biological standpoint, legal conditions can

only be *anomalous conditions*, as partial restrictions upon the actual life-will, which is a will for power.[85]

Nietzsche believed that if we consider the nature of life, and survey our daily experience through the lens of life, then we will find that the moral principles of refraining from hurting others, refraining from lying, refraining from treating people with injustice, refraining from exploiting and using people for one's own selfish ends, are to a significant degree inconsistent with our biology and with our living nature. If one is to flourish, one must live in a manner beyond good and evil.[86] This reflection led Nietzsche to associate traditional morality with weakness, decay, and death, for such traditional moral values, he believed, express the weakening of life and health.

In addition to being a philosopher of freedom, Nietzsche was a philosopher of health, and he regarded himself as a spiritual healer. He was nauseated by sickness as much as he was inspired by health. If there is any fatal flaw in Nietzsche's thought, it is that his hatred for sickness frequently overwhelmed him. He encapsulated his views on traditional morality in the following remark:

> Life itself requires us to produce values, and when we produce values, life values through us ... From this it follows that even the morality that goes against nature, which considers God as the opposing-concept and judgment against life, is only another value judgment of life itself – but which life? which type of life? – Well, I've already given the answer: that of the downward-going, weakened, tired and convicted life.[87]

The tougher facts of life: the will to power

As Nietzsche examined the nature of life more probingly, he searched for a principle whose expression could explain all of

life's manifestations, and could explain them neutrally, scientifically, and without any distorting moral sentimentality or bias.
Inspired by Schopenhauer's position that the essence of reality is
"will," Nietzsche developed his views on the nature of life by
adapting and modifying Schopenhauer's ideas to his own philosophical interests. He was also inspired by early Greek philosophy,
and in particular by the earliest Greek philosopher, Thales
(624–547 BC). At the beginnings of Western philosophy, there was
a search for a single principle of the cosmos – a single kind of
substance – whose transformation could explain the multitude of
things we experience. Thales understood the entire cosmos to be
transformations of water. Nietzsche, writing many centuries later,
hypothesized that the cosmos could be understood as transformations of the expansion of power, or as the "will to power":

> Now listen to my word, those of you wisest ones! Seriously
> examine whether I have crawled into the very heart of life, right
> into the roots of its heart!
>
> Where I found the living, there I found will to power; and even
> in the will of the subservients, I found the will to be ruler.
>
> That the weaker should serve the stronger – his own will
> convinces him of this, such that he wants to be ruler over even
> weaker ones: this pleasure alone he has no desire to renounce. And
> as the smaller gives itself up to the greater, so that it can have plea-
> sure and power over the smallest, so does the greater give itself up
> as it risks its life for more power. That is the sacrifice of the greatest
> – it is a risk and danger, and a dice-throw towards death.[88, 89]

> Physiologists should think twice before positing the instinct of
> self-preservation as an organic being's cardinal instinct. Above all, a
> living thing wants to *vent* its power – life itself is will to power: self-
> preservation is only its indirect and most frequent consequence.[90]

> To me, life itself is an instinct for growth, for endurance, for an
> amassment of forces, for *power*: where the will to power is deficient,
> there is decline. My claim is that this will is deficient in all of the

> highest values of humanity – that under the holiest names, values
> typical of decline, *nihilistic* values, have been leading the way. [91]

To explain human behavior, Nietzsche suggested that we think in terms of our behavior as being driven, owing to its living nature, by a desire for power of one kind or another. For him, the will to power is not a drive to reach a finally reconciled, steady-state, relatively happy and contented condition; it is a never-ending, insatiable push towards ever-expanding horizons, greater and greater control, and stronger and stronger constitutions. In his strong sense of purpose and self-discipline, and despite his artistic sophistication and culture, Nietzsche possessed a battle-friendly mentality – one that celebrated traditional warrior-values and people who are not afraid to engage in dangerous conflicts and expansive enterprises. He believed that extending one's horizons, even if by force, and even if it spells one's death, is a part of life and is an expression of health.

A strong will to power can be expressed in various ways, however, and Nietzsche reserved his greatest respect for those who express the will to power at the more refined levels of character-strength, dedication to a goal, consistency of will, and eagerness to overcome oneself, to "outdo" oneself, and to liberate oneself from external and internal limitations. Brutality, cruelty, and outrageous violence, although not absolutely dismissed, are not typically highlighted within Nietzsche's conception of the strongest-willed people. Consider his characterization of Socrates: "When the physiognomist had revealed to Socrates who he was – a cave of bad desires – the great ironist let out an additional word that gave the key to his character. 'This is true,' he said, 'but I became master over them all.'" [92]

There is an undeniable theme of "might makes right" – or rather, "health makes right" – that attends Nietzsche's celebration of life, but there is also the more amenable idea of standing primarily in competition with oneself, and not with others. Nietzschean health has much to do with being able to change, to adapt, and ultimately to transcend oneself – to revalue all of one's own personal values, and thereby metamorphose into a stronger and more enhanced being, much as does a caterpillar when it changes into a butterfly. "Death" and "resurrection" are acknowledged here, but Nietzsche acknowledges them as happening on earth, in practical, real-life terms. That is, a person of strong will-to-power is in a self-liberating position to revise completely his or her fundamental life project, and thereby become a person who is "reborn."

Nietzsche speculated that the idea of power, as an interpretive principle, could be extended beyond biological phenomena, and could be used to understand the entire cosmos. This brought him full circle to the point where Schopenhauer began his philosophy. Nietzsche did not initiate his philosophy, as did Schopenhauer, from a core metaphysical theory from which one could develop explanations of biological behavior by implication. Rather, he started from observations of how people and life operate, and generalized these to develop a vision of the universe. His resulting view did intersect with Schopenhauer's, since both regarded the universe as the manifestation of "will," in one form or another. Schopenhauer definitively and literally considered the world to be such; Nietzsche considered the world to be "will" more tentatively and interpretively. In the following excerpt from Nietzsche's notebooks, we encounter an interpretation of the world in terms of the will to power – one inspired by Schopenhauer, in conjunction with Nietzsche's studies of early Greek cosmologies. It describes what the world was for Nietzsche, as opposed to describing with rock-solid certitude how the world definitely is for us all, or how the world is in itself:

> Do you know what "the world" is to me? Shall I show it to you in my mirror? This world: a monster of energy, without beginning, without end, a solid, iron measure of force, which becomes neither more nor less, that does not use itself up, but only transforms; as a

whole, of unchanging size, a household without costs and losses, but also without growth, without revenues; surrounded by "nothingness," as by a boundary ...: this, my *Dionysian* world of the eternally self-creating, of the eternally self-destroying, this mystery-world of dual-sensuality, this, my "beyond good and evil" – without purpose, unless there is a purpose in the joy of the circle, without will, unless a ring has good will towards itself. Do you want a *name* for this world? A *solution* for all of its riddles? A *light* also for you, you most-hidden, strongest, most courageous, most midnightly ones? *This world is the will to power – and nothing besides!* And you too, are this will to power yourselves – and nothing besides![93]

The neutral and uncaring nature of Nietzsche's universe is striking, as it continually recycles, and goes essentially nowhere. This universe is mostly devoid of human qualities, and Nietzsche calmly gazes down on its turbulence as if he could see it from a distance, even as he, Friedrich Nietzsche, remained thoroughly intertwined within its meaningless twists of dice-throwing fate. The coolness and the psychological distance exhibited here is not unlike the standpoint he took towards the earth and human beings twelve years earlier, in the opening lines of his essay, "On Truth and Lie in a Morally-Disengaged Sense":

In some isolated corner of the cosmos, poured out shimmeringly into uncountable solar systems, there was once a star upon which clever animals invented knowledge. It was the most arrogant and hypocritical minute of "world history": but it was only a minute. After nature drew a few breaths, the star grew stiff with cold, and the clever animals had to die.[94]

Nietzsche often surveyed the human condition from the perspective of geological and astronomical time, where in the larger scheme of things, the human species has been in existence for less than the blink of an eye, and where the length of an individual's lifetime is so short as to approach the infinitesimal. As we extend our imagination in both directions, into the infinite past and future, human existence shrinks to a point, just as the earth shrinks to a point as one regards it from greater and greater spatial distances. Rather than marvelling at how such infinite and infinitesimal magnitudes can be imagined and experienced at all by those consciously-animated human specks of dust that crawl, apparently meaninglessly, on the earth – and such an intellectual feat seems almost miraculous – Nietzsche was usually content to look down on the human condition, as he pondered the significance of life within an emotionally cold universe that does not seem to care. Nietzsche's preoccupation was to determine the extent of human significance when, objectively speaking, from the standpoint of an infinite time and space, it seems to have virtually none.[95]

Considerations of this imaginative magnitude introduce the problem of evil in another guise, if we follow Nietzsche in assuming that there is no God and no moral balance to be hoped for, either in this world or in an afterlife. From this atheistic angle, the problem of evil is no longer the problem of how God can allow evil to happen; it is the more frightening problem of how to say "yes" to a world where there is no God to work against evil, and where there is no justice. In both formulations, we are forced to come to terms with evil, and it is in the face of such supposed realities that Nietzsche nonetheless aims to say "yes" to the world.

Nietzsche wanted to consider the most abysmal thought, the most dangerous thought, the most psychologically threatening thought, the most personally disintegrating thought, and then, under this deathly, "worst-case scenario" perspective on the world – a perspective where, objectively speaking, we are all alone in an uncaring universe ruled by nothing more than meaningless chance – test his strength to see whether he could still dancingly, joyfully, and thrillingly say "yes" to existence under such unpromising and uncompromising conditions. Such a thought experiment would be perverse, if it were not possible that the universe is intrinsically meaningless. Nietzsche thus wanted to test himself, to see whether his constitution was strong enough to have a perfectly good life while living permanently and finally in nothing less than pandemonium. Anyone who can do this would earn the title of being superhealthy.

When formulated in the above manner, it might be thought that the kind of being who would have an enjoyable time in pandemonium would be a naturally rebellious, defiant, Satanic being, and that in order to say "yes" to life, one would need to become unreflectively and unconscionably devilish and immoral. Nietzsche asserts that life is immoral, so if one intends to live in accord with what life dictates, then it would appear that one should act immorally and enjoy it.[96] This seems logically straightforward, but it cannot be the end-all expression of Nietzsche's prescription. If the goal is to interpret the world pandemonically as a way to test one's strength, then there will only be a test if one is a fundamentally moral being to begin with. For instance, a more demanding test of strength, and the greater tension within the soul, would be found in the saint who has been condemned to hell, or condemned to prison, rather than in the satanic being or true criminal. For the latter types, living in hell or in prison is less of a challenge, since they are at home there.

The more pressing problem for Nietzsche is how sensitive human beings can turn out well and live flourishingly in an inhuman universe, and not how sadists and masochists can flourish in a world of torture. Less dramatically, the problem is how a person who loves his or her parents can break away from them, live independently, and find themselves and their freedom; it is not the problem of how someone who is completely alienated from their parents can set out on his or her own.

The above situation of the sadists, masochists, and alienated ones – albeit reversed – is reminiscent of the view (sometimes ascribed to Kant) that a person who enjoys helping people by nature, and who is motivated only by those feelings of enjoyment, deserves less moral credit for his or her actions than someone who helps people out of a respect for reason, despite their having a predominantly inconsiderate and selfish character. The selfish person who does the right thing because it is required by duty deserves more moral credit, mainly because he or she does the right thing for the right reason. But it is also thought that this person deserves some extra moral credit, for he or she has done the right thing for the right reason as a consequence of an inner struggle which triumphed over selfishness. Using a similar logic in Nietzsche's case, the sadist or masochist, for example, who says "yes" to life, despite its pains, does not exemplify a person of great strength or power, for such a person is disposed to enjoy pain by nature.

What makes the difference, in terms of testing one's strength, is that the hellish environment – the daily world of suffering – is regarded as a difficult place in which to live, while it remains a place within which one can possibly thrive. This suggests that Nietzsche's philosophy is designed more for caring and culti-vated, yet potentially very strong-willed people, as opposed to those who are insensitive, coarse, and brutal, if only because the latter are more easily adaptable, and suffer less, under cruel, inhuman conditions.

Since brutal people have less to overcome in brutal contexts, they are like their mirror-opposite described in the Kantian example above, namely, the person who is helpful by nature, who experiences no struggle to do the right thing. Within this logic, neither deserves much credit for their actions, because they simply act as they are naturally disposed to act. Such people who are naturally akin to their environments have less to overcome, and are deprived of many spiritual trials that would allow them to grow. If one becomes too friendly with pain, or if one becomes desensitized to it, then the pain can no longer act as an obstacle. On this view, the most healthy people – those who have the highest expressions of the will-to-power – are, to the contrary, beautiful, yet hearty:

> And through what, fundamentally, does one recognize *the condition of having turned out well*? That a turned-out-well person does well for our senses: that he is cut from wood that is hard, delicate, and smells good at the same time. His taste is only for what is beneficial for him; his pleasure and his joy cease, when he oversteps that measure of what is beneficial. He guesses the cures for harmful things, he uses bad luck to his advantage; what does not kill him, makes him stronger. [97]

The religion of life: the eternal recurrence

The idea of "eternal recurrence" – the endless recycling of all that is, with the recognition of nothing beyond this recycling – issued from one of Nietzsche's major epiphanies, and he referred to it as the "highest formula of affirmation that is at all attainable."[98] For him, if one is able to believe in eternal recurrence – and believe it quite independently of whether it happens to be provably true – then one will embody a healthy attitude towards life and existence. Nietzsche's belief in eternal recurrence reflects his unconditional faith in life and existence itself.

What, then, would be healthy according to this doctrine? The healthiest attitude would be to enthusiastically affirm even the worst that life can offer, simply because this is a part of life. It would be to acknowledge pain, sickness, old age, lamentation, grief, despair, and imperfection, all to the point where the imperfect becomes perfect, because what in fact is, is accepted as what ought to be. It would be to love life and existence so much, that no matter what life or existence happened to do, one would love that fate unconditionally, just as one unconditionally loves one's own child, or just as God, as traditionally understood, unconditionally loves all of his creation. The attitude is one of complete and positive acceptance, and it is not merely the joyful wallowing in an abstract feeling of "life itself," but an emotionally-complicated acceptance and immersion into the concrete reality of life in every infinitesimal detail:

> *The heaviest weight.* – What if, some day or night, a demon were to crawl after you into your loneliest loneliness and say to you: "This life, just as you now live it and have lived it, you will have to live again, and innumerable times once more; and there will be nothing new in it, but rather every pain and every pleasure and every thought and sigh, and everything unspeakably small or great within it, must come back to you, and everything in the same order and succession – even this spider and this moonlight between the trees, and even this moment and I myself. The eternal hourglass of existence is turned over again and again, forever – and you along with it, speck of dust!"
>
> Would you not throw yourself down, gnash your teeth, and curse the demon who spoke in this way? Or have you once experienced a colossal moment, where you would have answered him: "You are a god and I have never heard anything more godlike!" If this thought were to take control of you, it would transform you as you are, or perhaps chew you to bits. The question in each and every thing: "Do you want this again, and even countless times again?" would lay upon your actions as the heaviest weight! Or how positive must one's attitude be towards oneself and towards life in order *to want nothing more* than this final, eternal confirmation and seal? [99]

Two centuries before Nietzsche lived, René Descartes (1596–1650) grounded his philosophy on a thought-experiment comparable to the one above.[100] Like Nietzsche, Descartes postulated an "evil demon" – one who was so powerful that he could make Descartes unsure of almost every thought he had, including apparent indubitabilities such as "2+2=4." With some further reflection on Descartes's part, the demon soon dissolved and transformed. For Descartes encountered in his mind the idea of a benevolent God that had been waiting to be discovered, like the stamp of an artisan upon his product.

Both Descartes's and Nietzsche's philosophies locate us initially in the realm of the demonic, and they eventually bring us into contact with the divine. Both philosophers move their readers from Hell to Heaven – from the dark night of the soul to a vision of the divine – although their respective conceptions of these opposing realms radically differ. Descartes believed that a divine realm exists beyond the world we live in; Nietzsche believed that "hell" and "heaven" are alternative interpretations of our ever-present world, depending upon whether one is weak-minded or strong-minded.

Nietzsche's doctrine of eternal recurrence is an existentialist doctrine – it is a doctrine which, if affirmed, intends to bring a person's attitude down to earth and render it more realistic. It can be regarded also as a direct attack on the belief in an otherworldly God – a belief which allegedly directs a person's significance towards a world beyond the present one, and which focuses one's attention and ultimate meaning in a world more perfect, moral, and tranquil than the one we happen to have. For Nietzsche, the belief in such an otherworld is a life-sapping illusion that leads us quickly to forget that we are at this very moment alive, and he prescribes the most this-worldly view he can imagine as a psychological countermeasure.

In his later years, Nietzsche spoke disparagingly of those who lacked the attitude appropriate to the affirmation of eternal recurrence – those whom he perceived everywhere around him –

referring to them as "failures-from-the-start," and ascribing to them an array of distasteful sentiments:

> Where does one not meet that covered-up look which burdens one with a deep sadness, that turned-inward look of the failure-from-the-start, which betrays how much a person talks to himself – a look, which is a sigh! "If only I could be someone else!" so sighs this look: "but there is no hope. I am who I am: how could I ever get free from myself? And indeed – *I am fed up with myself!*"
>
> It is upon such a ground of self-contempt, on such marshy ground, that every weed, every poisonous plant grows, and always so small, so hidden, so dishonest, so sickly sweet. Here wriggle the many worms of bitter resentment; here the air reeks of secrecy and guilty concealment; here is spun continually the web of the most malignant conspiracy – the conspiracy of the suffering against the well-turned-out and victorious; here, the aspect of the victorious is *hated*.[101]

Nietzsche's task was to discover and adopt a healthy interpretation of the world – one that would dissolve one's anger with the constraints of time and frustrations of past experience – and the doctrine of eternal recurrence was his final choice and concluding faith. The provable truth of this doctrine remains of secondary importance. What Nietzsche offered as something to "live for" – something he believed is expressed well by the doctrine of eternal recurrence – is the idea of living for life itself. The meaning of life is nothing beyond the experience of life as lived right now; it is a meaning that resides in the drama of life, and in nothing more. Just as a children's game has no other point outside the drama and fun of the game, Nietzsche believed that life has no other point outside of the game, outside of the stage, outside of the theater, of life.

Sometimes Nietzsche formulated this position with a focus on our own lives, here and now; sometimes he spoke abstractly, prophetically, and ideally about a general state of being – a kind of super-health – that is embodied by the *Übermensch* or "superhuman being".[102] Since life is best conceived of as child's play, insofar as life is art, and art is a kind of play, "being alive," "being playful," and "being theatric" all coalesce for Nietzsche. To be "superhuman" is to be able to affirm the belief in eternal recurrence, insofar as this is a doctrine of superlative health. It is also to carry oneself with the innocence of a child, with the many roles and perspectives of an actor, with the creativity of an artist, and yet with willpower as strong and as set as a rock.

The ideal of life: being in superhuman health

As we have seen, "life" is a foundational concept in Nietzsche's thought, and his philosophizing revolves around what are essentially medical and therapeutic issues concerning sickness and health. Although it may be melodramatic to say so, it would not be an exaggeration to note that Nietzsche conceives of his social project in the same general sphere as that of Buddha and Jesus. All three can be seen as cultural physicians who attempted to diagnose society's ills and to prescribe ways to become more spiritually healthy. All three, interestingly enough – and Nietzsche sometimes overlooked this point – are associated with conceptions of the divine as being located here on earth: the Buddha claimed to be nothing more than an ordinary human being; Jesus was in fact a human being considered to be the earthly embodiment or "son" of the divine; Nietzsche presented his *Übermensch* as a being that has a this-worldly existence, if it is to have any. Despite their differences, there is something down-to-earth and existentially-centered about them all, even though Jesus, on the face of things, represented the idea that there is another dimension beyond the present world where the absolute truth awaits.

Nietzsche's understanding of life as an immoral phenomenon, however, places his *Übermensch* in a philosophic region quite antagonistic to both Buddhistic and Christian expressions of spiritual health:

> Whoever has taken the trouble, as I have, to think deeply about pessimism with some puzzling desire, and to release it from the half-Christian, half-German narrowness and simple-mindedness with which it has been represented in this century, namely, in the figure of Schopenhauer's philosophy; whoever has, with an Asiatic and super-Asiatic eye, looked into and down into the most world-negating of all possible ways of thinking – beyond good and evil, and did so no longer, like Buddha and Schopenhauer, under the spell and delusion of morality – such a person may, without even wanting to, have awakened to the opposite ideal: the ideal of the most exuberant, life-filled, world-affirming person, who has not only learned to make peace with, and to tolerate, what was and is, but who wants moreover to have repeated throughout all eternity, just *how it was and is*, insatiably calling out "*da capo*," not only to himself, but to the entire performance and show. [103]

Since Nietzsche's vision aims toward revivification in all of its forms, he is not concerned with the human being *per se*, and he is unlike philosophers who centered their reflections upon the human being's supposed essence (often understood to be rationality or self-consciousness) and who then developed their philosophies on that anthropomorphic foundation. Nietzsche, as the unconditional worshipper of "life," is less concerned with the human being than with life in general. If the form of the human being needs to be modified, or even completely transcended, in order to enhance the expression of life energies on earth, then Nietzsche is content with that prospect. His descriptions of the superhuman state of being only sometimes refer to the human being's potentials, and in other instances, they refer to a being that will replace humans altogether.

Nietzsche's focus on "life itself" also explains why many of his remarks appear to be hard-hearted. The existence of each and every individual human being was not his main interest. He was concerned with life on earth, and if certain individuals do not exist in the service of this life, then his attitude towards them was unsympathetic. When, alternatively, he encountered particular individuals whom he believed to embody life itself, he tended to glorify them without much reservation. Nietzsche's god is life itself, and he loved all beings that are the children of life, some of which are found among the human species.

Some religious attitudes mirror Nietzsche's concerns about life, but they speak instead of "God" where Nietzsche speaks of "life," and speak of the "son of God," where Nietzsche speaks instead of "superhuman health." Since some say that "God is life," the affinity between the two concepts – "life" and "God" – reveals a structural kinship among these views. Nietzsche worshipped life in the unconditional way that some people worship God; he submitted his will entirely to life, just as some people submit their wills entirely to God. Nietzsche conceived of himself as both the servant to life and as the master of life. Some religious devotees conceive of themselves as the absolute servants to God, and as the pure embodiments of God's (or Heaven's, or Allah's, etc.) will thereby.

One could say, for instance, "Words that do not give the light of God increase the darkness,"[104] and formulate the related Nietzschean version, "Words that do not give the light of life increase the darkness," where the light of life is equivalent to health, and the darkness is equivalent to sickness. The two mentalities are akin, for they share an "all-or-nothing," "those who are not with me are against me," uncompromising, polarized style of thinking. A strong advocate of God might consider all non-God-supportive views as inherently "against" God, and as essentially benighted and spiritually lost; a strong advocate of life itself might consider all non-flourishing-supportive views as inherently "life-negating," and as essentially benighted and spiritually lost. The logic and psychologic is much the same.

There are nonetheless irreconcilable differences between Nietzscheanism and Christianity, or much more specifically, between Nietzsche and Schopenhauer (whom Nietzsche regarded as a voice of Christian morals). But it should not be overlooked how Nietzsche's philosophy accentuates the presence on earth of "God-as-life-itself" in the form of the superhumanly healthy state of being, and how the idea of "life itself" assumes a quasi-transcendent, or unconditional, status within Nietzsche's *Weltanschuung* under the title of what is "Dionysian." If there is any absolute, or categorical, or unconditional, imperative in Nietzsche's philosophy, it is: "Be healthy, whatever the moral cost!," or more familiarly, "Say 'yes' to life!" The superhuman being lives according to, and exemplifies, such an imperative of health. To look into the face of a superhuman being is to look into the eyes of life itself. To be a Nietzschean superhuman is to be life itself.

To appreciate further Nietzsche's oppositional relationship to Christianity, we can consider, by analogy, two different kinds of visual relationships. The first is the relationship between a photograph and its negative; the second is the relationship between two photographs of different, unrelated subjects. The first pair – the photograph and its negative – are strongly "opposite," and yet they remain isomorphic in structure; the second pair – two photographs of different things – are "opposite," insofar as they are of different things, and yet their opposition is less intense. Nietzsche's relationship to Christianity is analogously closer to the first, positive–negative image. He contradicts Christianity more than he runs merely contrary to it. For him, Christianity (more specifically, belief in the otherworldly Christian God), is not just another religious view among several hundred possibilities; it is the unhealthiest and most debilitating view.

Nietzsche, accordingly, formulated a distinctly anti-Christian view that aimed to be at the opposite end of the spectrum of world-views. His thought remained very closely connected to Christian thought, if only by being so directly opposed to some of Christianity's central tenets. He is a thinker who was hardly indifferent to Christianity, and he never ignored it. In this respect, Nietzsche never fully overcame Christianity insofar as he defined himself so squarely against it. From one perspective, one could say that without Christianity, there could be no Friedrich Nietzsche; from another perspective, one could say that without Christianity, there would be no need for Nietzsche. One can also wonder, though, what would be left of Nietzsche's philosophy, if we were to dissolve the Christian backdrop, or dissolve the shadows of God, against which it so sharply defines itself.

This close, but oppositional, relationship to Christianity that Nietzsche's views bear is expressed in the very last lines of *Ecce Homo*, his autobiographical work written during his last year of clear intellectual awareness:

Have I been understood? – *Dionysus versus the Crucified*.[105]

In his notebooks of the same year, he elaborated on his meaning:

The two types: Dionysus and the Crucified. – To ascertain: whether the typical *religious* person is a *form* of decadence (the great innovators are, as a lot, diseased and epileptic); but are we not here leaving out one type of religious person, the *pagan*? Isn't the pagan cult a form of thanksgiving and affirmation of life? Mustn't its highest representation be an apology and deification of life? The type of a well-turned-out and delightfully overflowing spirit! The type of spirit that assimilates whatever is contradictory and questionable in existence, and *redeems* it!

Here I put the *Dionysus* of the Greeks: the religious affirmation of life, the whole of life, with nothing denied or separated off; (typical – that the sex act arouses profundity, mystery, reverence).

Dionysus versus the "crucified": there you have the contrast. It is *not* a difference with respect to martyrdom – it is only that the martyrdom has a different sense. Life itself – its eternal overflowing and return – produces agony, destruction and the will towards extermination. In the other case, suffering – the "crucified as the guiltless one" – counts as an objection to this life, as the formula for its condemnation.

One can guess: the problem is about the meaning of suffering, whether it has a Christian sense or a tragic sense. In the former case, it is intended to be the way to a holy being; in the latter case, *being is counted as holy enough*, to justify even a tremendous amount of suffering. The tragic person affirms even the most severe suffering: he is strong, full, and deifying enough for it; the Christian negates even the happiest lot on earth: he is sufficiently weak, poor, disinherited, to suffer from life in every form of it he encounters. The god on the cross is a curse against life, an indication to be redeemed from it; – Dionysus broken into pieces, though, is a promise of life: it will be eternally reborn and will return home from destruction.[106]

Nietzsche was not so thoroughly dependent upon Christianity as to mechanically invert, in an act of defiance and negation, traditional Christian doctrines and values in a crude way, saying "yes" whenever Christianity said "no." He probably would have chuckled at those who practice a certain form of witchcraft, and rebel against Christianity by reading the Mass backwards and by engaging in sexual activity on the altar. This amounts to a kitschy and sophomoric version of Nietzscheanism. Rather, Nietzsche, having a more sophisticated intellect and more refined aesthetic sensibility, developed an anti-Christian vision largely derived from early Greek philosophy, and exemplified the nineteenth-century longing for a revivification of the then-prevailing Christianity. Nietzsche's alternative to Christianity was more aristocratic, discriminating, and in company with the likes of playwrights such as Friedrich Schiller, and the German Romantic poets.

To achieve his super-iconoclastic end, Nietzsche devoted much of his writing to invalidating the dictatorial authority of God, comparable to the way in which Martin Luther (1483–1546) initiated the Protestant Reformation by invalidating the interpretive authority of the priests. Both sought to free people from the yoke of oppressive religious dictation. Nietzsche, who was a more radical thinker, offered what he believed to be a liberating interpretation of the world as being ruled not by an otherworldly and absolutely determining moral judge, but by sheer accident. And in tune with this interpretation, he advanced a view of the cosmos as ever-circulating and recycling – one reminiscent of the early Greek philosopher, Anaxagoras, who hypothesized that the world rotates and recycles eternally – that allowed for a more down-to-earth, existential awareness, free of determination from another mysterious and unknowable source beyond our ken.

Nietzsche's *Übermensch* has been regarded by interpreters alternatively and mutually inconsistently, as an unrealizable ideal, as an actually coming reality, as a being completely indeterminate, as a being very specifically defined, as a being brutal and cruel, and as a being benevolent and enlightened. This variation in interpretation notwithstanding, one thing is clear: Nietzsche's superhuman being is the epitome of extraordinary health, and it stands as a heroic inspiration for the strong.

Across his career, Nietzsche upheld a variety of heroes, which included Schopenhauer and Wagner, and each directed the themes of his philosophizing at the time. When Nietzsche's idealization of Schopenhauer and Wagner faded in the late 1870s, he sculpted his own heroes on paper, in theory and in principle, and his eventually-arising *Übermensch* stands as the culmination of that effort to create his own super-person. In the following description, written during Nietzsche's final year of activity, the superhuman is described as embodying the healthy ideal of being perfectly "well-turned-out," although the superhuman is not to be confused with the "saint" or the "genius":

> The word "superhuman," as typically marking the highest level of being well-turned-out, in contrast to "modern" people, to "good" people, to Christians and other nihilists – a word, that in the mouth of Zarathustra, the exterminator of morality, becomes a very deep-thinking one – has with complete innocence, been understood almost everywhere in reference to those very values whose opposite the figure of Zarathustra was intended to offer: that is, as an "idealistic" type of a higher kind of person, half "saint," half "genius."[107]

Nietzsche's idea of the *Übermensch* does not appear explicitly in his writings until 1883, with the composition of *Thus Spoke Zarathustra*.[108] But his idea did not arise out of the blue. Several years before *Zarathustra*, he was engaged in formulating an ideal type which would serve the purpose of being the beacon of his philosophical outlook. Given how Nietzsche sometimes portrayed the *Übermensch* in opposition to Christianity, one might also believe that his conception of the superhuman is expressive of a completely secular, anti-Christian outlook, which is not sympathetically related to traditional religious imagery. As late as 1879, though, Nietzsche was still thinking positively of the churches as the setting for his philosophic-cultural vision, as can be seen in the following remarkable quote:

> *A vision.* – Hours of teaching and reflection for adults, for the mature and most mature, and these daily, without pressure, but attended by everyone as a rule of custom: the churches as the most worthy and most memory-filled places for this: a festival every day, so to speak, of the achieved and achievable dignity of human reason: a new and fuller blossoming of the ideal of the teacher, in which the minister, the artist and the doctor, the person of knowledge and the person of wisdom are all melted together, such that

their individual virtues are amalgamated into a single, total virtue, to be expressed in their teaching, their presentations, and their methods – this is my vision, which always returns to me, and which I firmly believe lifts a corner of the veil of the future.[109]

After 1879, Nietzsche began his wanderings though southern Europe, and brought his conception of the ideal culture more in line with his ever-deepening understanding of life – one that he soon recognized as necessarily involving pain, violence, exploitation, aggression, hostility, and many other qualities deemed "immoral" by society at large and by the traditionally-prevailing moralities. So in 1880, Nietzsche's "war on morality" properly began, and he subsequently developed a pronounced antagonism towards Christianity, losing more and more respect for the established Church as time went on.[110] As the above excerpt also indicates, though, Nietzsche's interest in improving the cultural situation – one expressed as early as 1872 in *The Birth of Tragedy* – carried religious and festival-related overtones, and it is mainly due to the evolution in his conception of life, as continually inspired by his studies of ancient Greek culture, that his perspective drew further away from the Lutheran outlook which had been the soul and substance of his forefathers.

As Nietzsche arrived at the distinct conclusion that "God" and "life" were opposed, he developed a position whose aim was to lead people out from the "shadows of God" into what he considered to be the noonday sunlight, just as Plato tried to lead people out of the dark cave of flickering shadows within which he believed we are all naturally chained in illusion. What Plato saw as illusion – the spatio-temporal, earthly world of fiery flux and day-to-day transformation – was, however, Nietzsche's core reality, and what Plato saw as reality – the world of unchanging, absolutely stable ideas – was Nietzsche's realm of predominant illusion, which he associated with the dream-world of Apollo. In their respective pursuits for enlightenment, Nietzsche and Plato walked in opposite directions, and as he condemned Christianity as "Platonism for the people," Nietzsche looked away from that religious perspective as well. Nietzsche's truth was revealed as a matter of concrete perception, willpower, and "being honest" about what the world presents in daily experience; Plato's truth was revealed as a matter of intelligible conception and reflection, and as a matter of seeing idealistically and perfectingly past the changing appearances to a flawless world beyond.

As time passed, nothing impressed Nietzsche more than the transcience of our daily world, along with its apparently senseless suffering. To this extent, he and Buddha would have made good friends. But Nietzsche wanted to live with the flame of suffering rather than extinguish it, and to this end, he interpreted the world as will-to-power, and advanced the doctrine of eternal recurrence. He set forth an ideal of superhuman health which, if realized, would allow a person to affirm life's suffering rather than seek refuge from it either by means of hopeful fantasy, or by means of meditational inner retreat. Nietzsche regarded such sanctuaries as spiritual anaesthetics, and the way of the anaesthetic was not his healthy way.

To understand the psychology of the Nietzschean superhuman personality, we can recall one of the most basic themes in Nietzsche's thought, namely, the question of whether or not life is worth living. Nietzsche's resounding "yes" to this question is formulated in a battling reaction to the acknowledged tragedy of life, and this Nietzschean problematic can be traced, in part, to his reflections on the tragedy of Oedipus. Specifically, Nietzsche notes in *The Birth of Tragedy* (§3), that in Sophocles's *Oedipus at Colonus* (lines 1224ff.), the Greek god, Silenus, presents King Midas with a statement of nihilism: it is best for people not to be born; the second best is for them to die soon, presumably because the world is too hellish and disappointing to make the effort worthwhile. In his crusade against nihilism, Nietzsche can be seen as an aspiring King Midas, or as a medieval alchemist, who tries to turn into gold even the lead-weight of a depressingly miserable existence.

Speaking generally, then, at one negative extreme is a particular kind of self-destructive, self-defeating, fundamentally suicidal, personality; at the opposite extreme is the superhuman, perpetually self-overcoming, personality. One can imagine a type of suicidal person who, whenever a standard "positive" event happened to him or her – a new job opportunity, a monetary benefit, a happy turn of events, a release from a previous difficulty – would interpret the event in an invalidating and defeatist light, such as to "make bad" out of what could be seen as positive, and to end up, ultimately, undermining his or her life altogether.

As an inverted mirror-image to the above type of suicidal, or defeatist, personality, one can imagine a fundamentally victorious person who, whenever a standard "negative" event happened to him or her, would immediately see the bright side, and interpret the event in a validating and conquering way, so as to "make good" out of what might ordinarily be seen as a crushing blow. Such a person would be excessively life-affirming and strong – as strongly positive as the suicidal person is negative. Such a life-affirming person would not do everything "in moderation," or worse yet, be lazy, sluggish, or thoroughly disinclined to hard work.[111] Simply put, the superhuman type is a "self-overcomer" who can make a healthy and heroic productive comeback from every personal disaster, even if this entails the complete restylization and consequent renunciation of his or her former self. Self-reconstruction requires self-destruction.

This is Nietzsche's imagined way to be, and it is why he says of the well-turned-out person, that "what does not kill him makes him stronger."[112] He wrote, quintessentially, a philosophy of fortitude, heroism, and victory – a philosophy which, if implemented, would help populate the world's stage with more dramatically meaningful and classically tragic characters. To achieve this, Nietzsche wrote a philosophy designed to overthrow those outworn, defeatist values that inevitably weigh heavy on people's minds; he wrote a philosophy aimed to cultivate more heroic characters for the universal theatre.

Nietzsche's superhuman being, in effect, appears in his screenplay as the lead theatrical player for an anticipated world performance, just as Dionysus once stood at center stage in classical Greek tragedy. Nietzsche's more modern performance is a bit more unnerving, however, for he locates it within a cosmic auditorium where only a single seat is set far back in the impenetrable shadows, to define the audience's place. In this seat, an unknowable God was once believed to have sat as the witness, spectator, and judge. In the anticipated performances of Nietzsche's heroic play, the seat is soon believed to be unoccupied. And finally, with a hollow laugh, the world-play is performed as if there had never been any hidden seat, witness, or all-seeing audience of one.[113]

5

Nietzsche's seduction of truth

Ravaging knowledge

Many believe that Nietzsche harbored antagonistic sentiments towards women, and a sufficient number of his remarks support this judgment. He did not, however, regard women in a uniformly negative light. It would be more accurate to observe that Nietzsche's attitude – as it was towards many subjects – was multi-aspected and context-variable. Moreover, some of his more well-known, and supposedly disparaging, remarks about women can be interpreted affirmatively, as sympathetic expressions of woman-associated forces that personify his own perspective. Nietzsche philosophized from the "perspective of life," and he claimed in the prime of his career that "life is a woman,"[114] so he can be said to have philosophized significantly from the perspective of woman. If we recall that Nietzsche believed that "life is immoral," and that he advanced this view as a more healthy and enlightened outlook, then some of his apparently negative comments about women – those which associate women with morally offensive qualities – reveal themselves to be supportive remarks, at least with respect to his own preferred values.

In *The Birth of Tragedy*, Nietzsche distilled the creative energies of Greek culture into two complementary and contending tendencies, the beautiful "Apollonian" and the terrific "Dionysian" forces. These two forces, he believed, were and are responsible for the development of art, "just as procreation depends on the duality of the sexes" (§1). His combination of the Apollonian and the Dionysian energies thus carried a subtle sexual overtone – one associated with the "duality" of the male and female sexes – although it remained tempered by the fact that Apollo and Dionysus are both male gods. Nietzsche's formulation of the Greek spirit in terms of male gods, and implicitly, in terms of male sexuality, is consistent with his views of ancient Greece, for he believed that the soul of Greek art was "a passion for naked *male* beauty."[115] Throughout *The Birth of Tragedy*, Nietzsche spoke predominantly in terms of a male–male style of opposing energies.

At one noteworthy juncture, Nietzsche departed momentarily from his natively Greek style of conceptualization and substituted in place of beautiful Apollo, the most satisfying dream-woman in the world, Helen of Troy. He referred to her as the redeeming and soothing force that rescues people from the direct sight of a terrifying world, and that sustains a strong and healthy attitude towards life:

> Here, nothing is reminiscent of asceticism, intellectuality or duty: only a luxuriant, even triumphant, existence speaks to us here, in which everything available is deified, whether or not it is good or evil. And so the observer may stand quite touched before this fantastic effusion of life, asking himself what magic potion was in the bodies of these high-spirited people, such that they could find life so enjoyable, that wherever they turned, they were met with the smile of Helen, the ideal picture of their own existence, "floating in sweet sensuality."[116]

One can interpret the beautiful Helen as representative of a nourishing and protecting mother-wife force – one that is positively supportive in a psychological sense, insofar as Helen is comparable to a benevolent and safeguarding "mother nature." To construct the polar opposite of this positive female force, one can replace the terrifying Dionysian force with a correspondingly feminized image, namely, that of the Medusa – the being who turns her beholders into stone.[117] In Nietzsche's writings, Medusa does not play a consistently highlighted role, and sometimes Nietzsche offers in the terrifying Medusa's place, the related and perhaps more revealing image of Baubo – a primitive and reputedly obscene female demon which was originally a personification of the female genitals.[118] In his 1886 preface to *The Gay Science*, Nietzsche wrote the following:

> "Is it true, that the Good Lord is present everywhere?," a little girl asked her mother: "But I think that's indecent" – a tip for philosophers! One should have more respect for the shame with which nature has hidden itself behind riddles and brightly dressed uncertainties. Maybe the truth is a woman, who has reasons for not letting her reasons be seen. Maybe her name is – to speak Greek – *Baubo*?
>
> Oh those Greeks! They knew how to *live*: for that, it is necessary to come to a brave standstill at the surface, at the drapery, at the skin, to worship the appearance, to believe in forms, tones, words, in the whole Olympus of appearance! These Greeks were superficial – *out of profundity!* And are we not exactly returning to this, we daredevils of the spirit, we, who have scaled the highest and most dangerous peak of contemporary thought, and looked around from there, we, who have *looked down* from there? Are we not exactly in that sense – Greeks? Worshippers of forms, of tones of words? And because of that – artists?[119]

In the concluding words above, Nietzsche links the artistic mentality with a respectful, reserved, and non-intrusive attitude – one that does not invade beneath the surface in its quest for truth, and which is content to find satisfaction on the more attractive and alluring surface. This artistic mentality is more disposed towards Helen than to either Medusa or Baubo, and it prefers the veiled truth, or even no truth at all, to the naked truth. Unlike the more coarse-minded philosophers and scientists who demand nothing less than the complete and literal truth, the artist desires that something be left to the imagination. Fourteen years earlier, Nietzsche expressed the same idea and the same reservations. Consider his statement in *The Birth of Tragedy*:

> At every uncovering of truth, the artist still attends to truth's outer wrappings with an enraptured gaze – he attends to that which remains even after the unveiling; whereas the theoretical person derives enjoyment from the wrappings to the extent that they are discarded, and has as the highest goal of his pleasure, the always-pleasant process of uncovering that has succeeded by means of his own forcefulness.[120]

These remarks reveal Nietzsche's mixed attitudes towards science, God, and the traditional quest for the truth. Nietzsche the philosopher and scientist aimed to uncover the truth of the world, whereas Nietzsche the artist had no taste at all for this fundamentally intrusive enterprise. Nietzsche both wanted and did not want the absolute truth, and his views on the value of metaphysical inquiry along with his views on women run in parallel: he wanted and did not want to dissolve the mystery that women presented to him.[121] There is a distinct sense in which Nietzsche often, and with great repulsion, regarded philosophers and scientists – to put the matter baldly – as the bullies and ravagers of reality, because their unconditional quest for truth violates nature's secrets.

Nietzsche's more respectful attitude towards truth and women can be gleaned from the initial remarks in the quotation above, where he speaks of the "indecency" of God's knowledge of everything. Here, Nietzsche conceives of God as exemplifying a principle comparable to that of the scientist: both are engaged in "knowing everything" such that all secrets, all intimacies, all mysteries, all soothing illusions, and all innocence, are laid completely bare, whether or not these secrets ought or ought not to be known. Lest this sound extreme, let us recall what Nietzsche's "ugliest man" said at one point about his need to "kill God":

> But he ... *had* to die: he saw with eyes that saw everything – he saw the depths and grounds of people; he saw all of their hidden humiliation and ugliness. His pity had no shame: he creeped into my dirtiest corners. This absolutely-curious, too-intrusive, too-pitying one had to die. He *always* saw me: I wanted to have revenge on such a witness – or else not live. The God who saw everything, *everyone included* – this God had to die! A person cannot stand it, that such a witness should live.[122]

Nietzsche's attack on the scientific attitude, his call for the death of God, and his rejection of "truth" can all be linked to his "artist's" attitude of respecting the illusory, superficial, and enveloping qualities of life, without which life would be meaningless. Part and parcel of this approach to the world is Nietzsche's 1886 suggestion that if "truth is a woman," and if one desires truth, then it should be "seduced" from the world, and gently coaxed away from mother nature, rather than stolen away by direct assault and disrespect. Insofar as he regarded God as an indelicate and inartistic invader, as a being whose panopticism robs everyone of their privacy, Nietzsche regarded himself, and every other human, as comparable to a woman whose respect has been violated by an aggressive and inconsiderate man. Hence we find Nietzsche seemingly protecting himself at one point:

> Everything that is deep, loves masks; the most profound things even have a hate for pictures and allegories. Should not the very opposite of this be the proper cover-up for the shame of a god?… It is not the worst things for which a person has the worst shame: there is not only fraudulency behind the mask – there can be plenty of kindness in being fraudulent. I can imagine that a person

who had something valuable and sensitive to protect, might roll through life in a coarse and round manner, like an old, green, heavily-weighed-down wine cask: the subtlety of his shame would require it.[123]

What immensely complicates the above, sensitive aspect of Nietzsche, is his further view that life itself – i.e., "mother nature" – is immoral, exploitative, invading, appropriative, and violent. Although life might be responsible for generating necessary illusions and might be an "artistic" force in that sense, life also operates fundamentally without the respect and decorum that Nietzsche complained is supposedly lacking in God. Nietzsche's attack on God reveals how he cared neither to have his privacy invaded nor his integrity undermined, and yet he also stressed that life itself is invasive and disintegrating, which is to say, metaphorically, that he fell in love with Helen's beautiful face, while he painfully acknowledged that this was really a mask for Baubo or Medusa. More philosophically, Nietzsche felt a deep sense of self, while he painfully acknowledged that this self, or ego, or subject of experience, or integrated personality, was, in the final analysis, without substance and doomed to disintegration by the very forces that created it. Helen and Baubo personify mother nature's appearance and reality, respectively, as soft and charming, and as ferocious and feral.

In *The Birth of Tragedy*, Nietzsche located the realm of suffering in the world of everyday objects and desires, and he found salvation from mundane individuality in two locales – in the beautiful, idealized world of dreaming illusion, and in the ecstatic immersion into the trans-individual forces of "life itself." In both, Nietzsche offered a retreat from the "real-life" world of suffering. As his career developed, his attitude grew more and more accustomed to, and disposed towards, the day-to-day world, complete with all of its imperfections and frustrations. A significant part of this development can be understood, if we consider in more detail, Nietzsche's "perspectivism," noting how his conceptions of truth and women developed in parallel with transformations in his perspectivist doctrine.

Amending reality's split

Nietzsche's views immediately following *The Birth of Tragedy* displayed a sharp awareness of the limits of the human perspective, for he observed how our particular sense organs allow us to glimpse only a small section of the universe. From 1872 to 1885, he claimed that "reality" or the "thing-in-itself" is either unknowable, or if it is knowable, is quite irrelevant to the construction, foundation, and legitimacy of human values. This is one of Nietzsche's central ideas: reality itself is mindlessly neutral with respect to human values; it does not care about how we evaluate things. Goodness, justice, and right are not part of the universe's human-independent fabric, and it is pointless to ask for a moral justification, or theodicy, that legitimates the suffering and "evil" in the world. Seeking a moral justification for life's sufferings is comparable to asking a block of ice why it fell and caused an avalanche. The ice block has no consciousness and it cannot respond; the block fell for mechanical reasons, or it fell by accident. Such is the entire human-independent world. For Nietzsche, the world simply is what it is, and he believes that we alone project our evaluations, positive or negative, upon the various things we experience, given our life-related interests. These projections remain only our evaluations, and in itself, the world is neither fair nor unfair, neither good nor evil, and neither benevolent nor cruel: "If becoming is a great ring, each and every thing is equally valuable, eternal, necessary. – In all co-relations of Yes and No, of acceptance and rejection, love and hate, there is only the expression of a perspective, of the interests of a certain type of life: in itself, everything that is, says Yes."[124]

We see here Nietzsche's "say 'yes' to life" dictum juxtaposed with a "reality is neutral" assumption. Strictly speaking, given the latter assertion of neutrality, one should not be saying "yes" to the world, but should remain neutral about the value of existence, adopting neither an over-joyous, ecstatic, universally affirming attitude, nor a discouraged, pessimistic, universally disconfirming one. This qualification notwithstanding, it is important to appreciate Nietzsche's concern with the question of whether or not values are infused into the heart of reality itself, especially in connection with the question of the meaning of suffering – the worry addressed by the traditional problem of evil. Nietzsche, while denying that values are intrinsic to the world as it is in itself, sets out to interpret life in a meaningful way nonetheless. His problem is how to live a life worth living, when the world is objectively valueless. His 1886 solution asks us to operate superficially and artistically as a way to maintain this value. If one thinks too hard about things and apprehends too much of the truth, previously constituted values will dissolve and things will become worthless. On this view, value depends upon illusion, whereas truth is revealed in the experience of becoming disillusioned. Insofar as "truth" is a value, there is no truth. Insofar as there is genuine truth, there are only valueless and trivial truths. Such is one important perspective that prevails across Nietzsche's career.

Throughout his writings up until 1885/86, Nietzsche wavered between maintaining that reality itself is unknowable and that its nature is therefore irrelevant to considerations of human value, and maintaining that reality is knowably neutral, and is therefore irrelevant to considerations of human value. The outcome is the same on both alternatives. At this time, he tended to recognize a distinction between "appearance" and "reality," believing that "reality" is value-neutral as far as we can be concerned, and might even be value-neutral in itself. For him, the most fundamental human interests do not coincide with objective cosmic workings. Nietzsche is clear about this in one of his note-book remarks from 1884:

> It is sufficient that the more simplistically and coarsely it is grasped, the *more filled with value*, the more definite, beautiful, and meaningful the world *appears*. The more deeply one looks into it, the more our evaluations dissolve – *meaninglessness draws near*! *We* have created the world that has value! Recognizing this, we also recognize that the reverence for truth is thereby the *effect* of an *illusion* – and that one should rather treasure the force that forms, simplifies, shapes, fabricates.
>
> "All is false! All is permitted!"
>
> Only with a certain bluntness of outlook, a will to ordinary simplicity, do beauty and the "valuable" present themselves: in itself, it is *I know not what*.[125]

Nietzsche's interpreters often understand his perspectivist outlook in reference to texts that he wrote between 1872 and 1886, when he often emphasized how our various perspectives keep us "in prison" (*Daybreak*, §117), with respect to the way the universe is in itself. The best we can do in such a limited situation, he then claimed, is to adopt as many perspectives as we can, to obtain an increasingly comprehensive understanding of the world. We will never reach the absolute truth, but this is not a problem for human meaning, because the truth of the cosmos is essentially irrelevant to our life-concerns, all of which issue from our finite human perspective and desire to live, and to live well.

Around the time of *Beyond Good and Evil* (1886), Nietzsche's views on the validity of the appearance-reality distinction, considered as a metaphysically basic distinction, began to erode.[126] In the works of 1885 and 1886, he started to question the distinc-tion, and he began hypothesizing how the world could be conceived independently of this dichotomy.[127] As part of this transformation, he questioned some closely related philosophical concepts such as the "thinking self" or "I" that supposedly precedes the thinking of some thought, and the "acting self" or "moral agent" that supposedly precedes some action as the intentional cause of that action.

These inquiries led Nietzsche to a position where he no longer talked about a set of different "perspectives," all of which were assumed to be about, or to be directed towards, some inscrutable reality. Rather, he imagined a set of perspectives *simpliciter*, without assuming any underlying reality, or any "thing-in-itself" which they each partially revealed, and partially veiled. In 1886, Nietzsche began to recognize our given, daily experience alone as being philosophically and existentially important, just as it stands – an experience which he believed is grounded upon a "medley of sensations," and which resists further division into the two abstracted, and metaphysical, dimensions of "appearance" and "reality," and to which one respectively coordinates "illusion" and "truth." In a notebook entry of 1887, we find a solid statement of what remained only tentative in his 1886 reflections:

> When one comprehends that the "subject" is not something that creates effects, but is only a fiction, all sorts of things follow.
>
> It is only in terms of the model of the subject that we have invented "thing-ness" and have laid this interpretation upon the chaos of sensations. If we no longer believed in the *effect-creating* subject, we would cease believing in the effect-creating things, in cause-and-effect reciprocity, in cause and effect between those phenomena that we call things.
>
> With this, naturally, the world *of effect-creating atoms* is dropped: the assumption of which one always makes under the precondition that subjects are brought in.
>
> Finally, the "thing-in-itself" is also dropped: because it is itself, fundamentally, the concept of a "subject-in-itself."[128] But we understand that the subject is a fabrication. The opposition between "thing-in-itself" and "appearances" is untenable; and with that, the concept of "appearances" drops away as well.[129]

Once the idea of an "absolute truth" is dissolved into the flux of human sensory experience, the traditional idea of associating "truth" with "stability" is equally dissolved. What, then, would be the "truth," if it were not something stable? During the last years of his intellectual development, Nietzsche preferred the phrase "creating truth" as opposed to "discovering" any fixed truth, and he took steps to associate the creation of truth with his fundamental doctrine of the "will to power." Insofar as people postulate values, and insofar as these postulated values are set forth as "truths," then it is only a matter of willpower that postulates "truths." To the extent that these "truths" are only postulations, they are subject to change. Moreover, to the extent that "all is in flux," there can only be such truth-as-postulation or truth-as-creative-positing:

> "Truth" is therefore not something that is there to find out, to be discovered, but something *that must be created*, and it names a process, or better yet, a will to dominate that has no end: truth is put forth as a *processus in infinitum*, an active determining – not a becoming-conscious of something that is solid and determined in itself. It is a word for the "will to power."[130]

The truth as a face in the clouds

The above excerpts recall how Nietzsche's views transformed during his last three years of intellectual activity. Up until 1886, he recognized a "truth" that exists independently of people, and tended to consider human beings, and all other life-forms as well, as beings confined within some perspective or other, never quite apprehending what is there as a "thing-in-itself," independently of all possible finite perspectives. In 1887 and 1888, however, he conceived of what "underlies" our organized world of sensory experience – the "truth" – as nothing fundamentally different in metaphysical kind from the sensory world, but only that very world conceived differently, namely, as a fluctuation of sensations: "the opposite of this phenomenal world is *not* 'the true world,' but the formless–unformulable world of the chaos of sensations – therefore *a different kind of* phenomenal world, which is for us 'unknowable.' "[131]

Nietzsche thus interpreted the traditional quest for the "true world" in line with a new and different understanding of perspectivism. Previously, as noted, he conceived of various "perspectives" on the world, as one would imagine the various perspectives held by a large set of people sitting around a table, all of whom all contemplate a vase placed at the table's center. In this situation, there is the central object, and a set of partial disclosures of that object, where we can say that each perceiver apprehends some of the object's "truth," or in the case of a very bad seating arrangement, cannot see much of the object at all.

Unlike the above model, Nietzsche's later concept of a "perspective" is closer to that of an "interpretation," and is more comparable to how an abstract line drawing that immediately looks like a cube can also be seen as a flat diamond shape. In terms of more philosophical examples, our world as experienced can be interpreted variously, as being a mechanistic series of atomized events, or a flow of energy, or a manifestation of some god's thoughts, or as a "slice" of a wider dimensional manifold, or as the "will to power," or as a set of colored, solid, "bigger-than-or-smaller-than-a-breadbox"-sized objects, among many possibilities. Throughout all of these interpretations, it is the "same" presented world of sensory experience that is being interpreted through these various imaginative angles, with nothing hidden from view. To characterize more aptly Nietzsche's later style of perspectivism, we can refer to it as "interpretationism" as opposed to "perspectivism," which can be reserved for his views of 1886 and before.[132, 133, 134]

Within this interpretationist standpoint, there is "experience" which is subject to many interpretations, and all efforts to go imaginatively beyond this always already interpreted condition, such as to experience "pure experience" or "experience itself," are impossible: it is inconceivable, so it now seems to Nietzsche in a more wide-ranging way, to extract oneself wholly from some interpretation or other, within which one is always already involved. The very ideas of "truth" and "objectivity" *en toto* are now believed to derive their meaning from within one's interpretation, as opposed to the more traditional assumption that they derive their meaning in reference to that which exists independently of all interpretations. The neutral "world-in-itself," towards which all of our interpretations are supposed be aimed, soon dissolves in our very reference to, and in our very act of, conceptualizing such a being. For what was once regarded as standing outside of all interpretations Nietzsche recycles and reinjects into the interpretation itself, leaving us philosophically suspended and without any unchanging foundations left to comprehend.

Nietzsche, then, becomes more thoroughly a "philosopher of flux" at the end of his career. Unlike his earlier theorizing, when he referred to something objective, but of which he "knew not what" it could definitively be, Nietzsche gravitated to a more earth-bound, experience-centered, fluctuation-emphasizing position, where the "testimony of the senses" – our direct experience without any conceptual overlay – became the best truth he could hypothesize:

With the highest deference, I exempt the name of Heraclitus. When the other philosophic-folk threw out the testimony of the senses because they showed that things display multiplicity and change, he threw out their testimony, because they displayed permanence and continuity. [But] Heraclitus also did an injustice to the senses. The senses neither lie in the way the Eleatics believed, nor as he believed – they do not lie at all. What we *make* out of their testimony, that is what puts in the lies, for example the lie of unity, the lie of thinghood, of substance, of permanence... We falsify the testimony of the senses because of "reason." Insofar as the senses display becoming, passing away and change, they do not lie. In that respect, Heraclitus is eternally correct to hold that being is an empty fiction. The "apparent" world is the only one: the "true world" is only an *added-on lie*.[135]

We have done away with the true world: which world is left to remain? The apparent world, perhaps? ... But no! *With the true world we have also done away with the apparent one!*

(Noon; moment of the shortest shadow; end of the longest mistake; high point of humanity; INCIPIT ZARATHUSTRA.)[136]

Nietzsche's concluding interpretationist view is that nothing remains metaphysically concealed, and that one can cut, slice, divide, expand, and stretch the world's contents as much as one desires, and there will always be only more of the same.[137] This is to say that the fluctuating, sensory world we are now in is all there is, which is to say that "this is it," and that there are no metaphysical secrets left except perhaps the secret that there are no metaphysical secrets. Even calling for the delicate "seduction" of the truth – Nietzsche's 1886 suggestion – does not capture this new situation, because there is no longer any "surface" that is to be distinguished from an underlying, hidden reality. It is more as if a completely masked and wigged personage were seduced to disrobe, and one were to discover nothing but empty space. Such a personage could not even be called "superficial," since there had never been any hidden, naked body beneath the clothing.[138] The truth is like an empty mask that hangs on a wall, and which has no flesh-and-blood face behind it. In 1888, Nietzsche spoke this way about women, saying that women are "not even shallow."[139] Rather than judging this to be a rude remark, it appears to be Nietzsche's identification of women with his conception of the nature of human experience.

We are thus presented in experience with a sensory surface that looks like a mask; we are presented with clouds in the sky that look like faces. We are presented with a painting of a rice-cake that we cannot eat, for the painting is made only of paint.[140] That there is a hidden truth waiting to be discovered behind this mask, or a cosmic intelligence waiting to be discovered behind these passing clouds, is an illusion. The mask is empty, the clouds are just clouds, and the sensory surface of our experience is only comparable to the surface of a painting. The world is a stage, and there is nothing hidden behind the sensational and sensory play. We act in our own exclusively human play, not realizing that we are the playwrights, believing that the meanings suggested by historical configurations were meant to be by a universal intelligence.

For Nietzsche, the thought that life's meaning is comparable to the meaning projected upon a cloud formation, or upon a wind-sculpted stone, or upon a set of happy coincidences was liberating. It defined a liberation similar to the experience of having once believed in a God who peered into one's soul, and then having later realized that this was only a face in the clouds, or a "man in the moon." It is a liberation that is Buddhist as well, for one reads in *The Tibetan Book for the Dead* (c. fourteenth century) that liberation is just like the experience of being terribly frightened by what appears to be a lion, only to realize later that one had been running away from nothing more than a stuffed lion-skin.[141]

In both Nietzscheanism and Tibetan Buddhism, the experience of liberation from oppressive forces and illusion is achieved similarly: one reinterprets the world so that what was previously regarded as having an independent existence is seen as one's own projection. Through an act of interpretation, one realizes that all along, one had only been afraid of one's greater self, having previously failed to see that the feared objects were only manifestations of the "it," or "other," or "id," within one's own psyche.

In Nietzsche's particular case, liberation arises on specifically accepting that the *value* and *meaningfulness* of the world derive from our own projection. Quite independently of the values we project, Nietzsche did acknowledge the independent reality of the daily world and he aimed to affirm it. And this realistic attitude distinguishes his outlook from many versions of traditional Buddhism, as well as from Kant and Schopenhauer – views which all accept the distinction between "appearance" and a metaphysically different "reality." Nietzsche nonetheless adopted the same basic strategy for personal liberation within his interpretationist outlook. Being able to see oneself reflected in what once appeared to be an independently existing world-presentation is their common path to liberation. The more we take responsibility for what we experience – the more we appreciate the power of our own creativity – the more we are liberated.

6

Embracing life versus embracing existence

Life-affirmation and the world's imperfection

Throughout his writings, Nietzsche oscillates between saying "yes" to life and saying "yes" to existence, often equating the two ideas and fusing them together in the same breath. In *The Birth of Tragedy*, for example, he questions the worth of existence as a whole, and he answers positively in terms of becoming one with life as a whole. At the end of his career, on the same note, he states in *Ecce Homo* that when one's attitude is healthy, one says "yes" to life, and acknowledges how this affirmation implies that one will desire that "nothing in existence may be subtracted." Life-affirmation and existence-affirmation are much the same thing for Nietzsche. That he continually expanded his conception of the will-to-power from an initially human-referring, to a life-in-general-referring, to an all-of-existence-referring concept, supports the idea that life and existence blended together in his mind, and that he believed that affirming one involves affirming the other.

To affirm life and to affirm existence, however, are different kinds of affirmation, with different and conflicting implications for one's attitude towards the world. The phenomena of life appear to be limited to the earth, and life on earth appears to have been present for only a relatively short amount of time, geologically and astronomically speaking. In contrast, existence itself extends immeasurably beyond the sphere of living things, both in space and in time. From one perspective – the very perspective from which Nietzsche looks down on the earth and human beings – life itself, not to mention human life in particular, amounts to only a brief twinkling of existence. There is a vast difference between life and the infinite totality of what exists.

Moreover, although Nietzsche is an existence-affirming thinker and has been faithfully characterized in histories of philosophy as an "existentialist," he is first-and-foremost a life-affirming thinker, as is evident through the many contexts within which he measures his surrounding world in terms of sickness and health. Nietzsche positively values what is healthy, and he tends to recoil from what is sick. He positively values existence, mostly because he regards adopting an existence-affirming attitude as an expression of health. He is more of a down-to-earth doctor of cultural ills, rather than a person who is awe-struck by the bare fact that he exists. The old and profound metaphysical question, "Why is there something rather than nothing?," is less important to Nietzsche than the practical question of what it means to be healthy, given that one is now here and alive. That he exists is more of a disturbing puzzle to him than an unqualified inspiration, given the imperfect world within which he was thrown, or out of which he grew.

One consequently discovers within Nietzsche's thought a perspectival fluctuation and tension between the attitudes of life-affirmation and existence-affirmation. More precisely, this tension exists between the "affirmation of *health*" and the "affirmation of existence." Insofar as Nietzsche is health-affirming, he speaks intolerantly towards certain aspects of existence, namely, those which he believes either foster or embody sickness and decline. He rants against Christianity, and he deprecates outlooks that assert the truth and desirability of universal equality, justice, and total peace, for he associates them with spiritual degeneration and weakness. Nietzsche, as we can so often see, has a difficult time affirming the recurring existence of the people who, according to his standards, are numbered among the weak:

> And the bite on which I choked the most, wasn't knowing that life necessitates hostility and death and torture-crosses: – but I once asked, and almost choked on my question: What? Does life also make the riffraff *necessary*? Are poisoned wells and stinking fires and dirty dreams and maggots in the bread of life necessary?[142]

> I once saw both of them naked – the greatest people and the smallest people – all-too-similar to one another; even the greatest was all-too-human. The greatest was all-too-small! – that was why I was so fed-up with people. And the eternal recurrence of even the smallest ones! – that was why I was so fed-up with all existence! Ugh, Nausea! Nausea! Nausea![143]

We can almost hear Nietzsche's fist slamming down on the table, as he contemplated the existence of sickness with such intolerance, and it is easy to speculate that there were times when he hated being physically unwell. Less personally, and more philosophically, such hard valuations derive from Nietzsche's predominant concern with being the champion of cultural health. His reflections are sometimes so severe as to suggest that the human species as a whole is so spiritually ailing, weak, and "all-too-human," that humanity as a whole "must be overcome." From this, in part, derive Nietzsche's references to the "superhuman being" that suggest that this being is not a human being.

As he says in the Prologue to *Thus Spoke Zarathustra*, the human being is "a rope, tied between beast and superhuman." Just as the ape is a "laughingstock or painful embarrassment" to the human being, so will the human being be a laughingstock or painful embarrassment to the superhuman being. Human beings will not inherit the earth, since humans as a whole are so unworthy; it is the superhuman being that will finally earn the right to carry "the meaning of the earth." This superhuman being is the most holy being to Nietzsche, and he suggests that to sin against it is the greatest sin. Thus speaks his main character, Zarathustra.

Nietzsche's despising evaluations can be multiply illustrated, and his well-intended preoccupation with health *per se* is largely responsible for their presence in his writings. Along another line of reflection, though, Nietzsche expands the scope of his affirming attitude to cover all existence, rather than only that which he recognizes as the healthy part. In such instances, his attitude towards the sicker and weaker forms of life noticeably softens, almost as if it were directed by his awareness of a purely logical implication: at a certain level of abstraction, if one decides to say "yes" to all existence, pure and simple, despite its contents, then existence is existence, and there is no better or worse of which to speak. Existence-affirmation has a greater value-levelling quality than does life-affirmation. If one measures the world in terms of life-as-health, then there are clearly better and worse levels of health, and one can speak meaningfully in degrees of something's being "half alive" or "barely alive"; if one measures the world in terms of existence, then there is more of an "all-or-nothing" quality to one's judgment. By choosing to affirm existence in general, one commits oneself to affirming all of it indiscriminately and equally. Of course, one need not become unaware of, or insensitive to, differences in quality thereby; one can accept imperfect situations wholeheartedly, recognizing them for the limited conditions that they are. But they will be differences that make no overriding difference to one's affirming attitude.

Just as Nietzsche's "ugliest man" – the murderer of God – could never overcome his guilt, because, despite the fact that he had "killed God," God-related values continued to persist in his memory, Nietzsche does not appear to have stepped significantly beyond the constraints of life-affirmation into his own perceived noontime daylight of existence-affirmation.[144] He was able to move from the traditional moral view to a life-affirming view, wherein the distinction between good and evil dissolved, so as to arrive at a standpoint "beyond good and evil." He was not, however, clearly able to move non-ambivalently and completely from a life-affirming to an existence-affirming view, so that the distinction between health and sickness dissolved, and it would be possible to affirm all existence, whether it was healthy or sick. Nietzsche made the transition from traditional morality to life-affirmation, but he continued to vacillate uneasily between the life-affirming view and the existence-affirming view, for he never stopped writing about the sick aspects of life, and never stopped being irritated by these imperfections. Nietzsche appears to have ended his career with some measure of frustration and dissatisfaction, because the sickness of the world, and probably of his own deteriorating body as well, continued to vex him.

Existence-affirmation and the world's perfection

On the more positive face of things, Nietzsche's existence-affirming discussions take us beyond his more discontented remarks towards a more thoroughly joyful outlook. When the doctrine of eternal recurrence is understood through health-affirming or "flourishing-affirming" eyes, the recurrence of the sick does become a point of difficulty.[145] When the doctrine is understood through existence-affirming eyes, though, then whatever happens is interpreted as an affirmative occasion, and sickness presents no obstacle. Sometimes Nietzsche assumed this latter attitude as well, even in his final year of intellectual activity, when his intellectual collapse was imminent:

> My formula for greatness in people is *amor fati*: that a person wants nothing different – not forward, not backward, not in all eternity.

It is not simply to cope with what is necessary, still less to hide it ... but *love* it.[146]

Even at this moment I can see my future – an *expansive* future! ... I do not want in the slightest, that anything become different than it is; I myself do not want to become different. [147]

Zarathustra is a dancer – : like one, who has the hardest, most horrible insight into reality, and who has thought the most "abysmal thought," without having it be an objection to existence, not even to its eternal recurrence. Moreover, one who finds a ground therein, *to make himself* into an eternal Yes to all things, "the awesome, unbounded Yes and Amen." "I still carry my beneficent affirmation into all abysses" – *But once again, that is the concept of Dionysus.* [148]

Such existence-affirming remarks are inspiring, but in general, it is rare to find Nietzsche lovingly reaching down to everyone who is sick, weak, and dying, as Jesus did. When we encounter Nietzsche saying "yes" to existence as a whole, or affirming eternal recurrence in a way that is not tinged with a distaste for the recurrence of the weak, his affirmation tends to reside at a very high, and noticeably distanced, level of abstraction, where he affirms not the details – not the scars, the breakdowns, the nauseas, the failures – but the cosmic recycling process in general. Nietzsche asserts that he loves "eternity," which is to say that he loves the entire world as "world-in-general," and he does not typically assert, as a rule, that he loves the infinitely detailed world.[149] And this abstract style of world-affirmation is a slightly disappointing departure from Nietzsche's generally discriminating and nuanced approach to his subjects. In his existence-affirming moments, he tended to speak only generally, just as he spoke generally of "life itself" in *The Birth of Tragedy* when he described the joyous nature of life-affirmation. His existence-affirming remarks are comparably indeterminate:

> O how could I not lust for eternity, and for the ring of all wedding rings – the ring of recurrence?
>
> I have not yet found the woman from whom I'd like to have children, but it would be this woman that I love: because I love you, o eternity!
>
> *Because I love you, o eternity!*[150]

This is a thought-provoking paragraph, and it is cited by some scholars as signifying Nietzsche's overcoming of the disgust he felt on considering the recurrence of the rabble, of the weak, and of the sick.[151] Here, Nietzsche professes to love existence as a man loves a woman, and he loves the particular cyclical style of existence – further idealized here as a wedding ring – as a person would find attractive the personality of his or her beloved. There is much that is romantic and dreamy about Nietzsche's love of existence, and his expressions of existence-affirmation convey an ecstatic quality. With respect to his association between eternity and woman, though, his attitude remains comparatively unrealistic, in contrast to the more down-to-earth kind of love Shakespeare expressed in Sonnet 130:

> My mistress' eyes are nothing like the sun;
> Coral is far more red, than her lips' red;
> If snow be white, why then her breasts are dun;
> If hairs be wires, black wires grow on her head.
> I have seen roses damasked, red and white,
> But no such roses see I in her cheeks,
> And in some perfumes is there more delight
> Than in the breath that from my mistress reeks.
> I love to hear her speak, yet well I know
> That music hath a far more pleasing sound;
> I grant I never saw a goddess go –
> My mistress when she walks treads on the ground.
>   And yet by heaven I think my love as rare
>   As any she belied with false compare.[152]

Shakespeare's characterization of his beloved is more existentially-guided and realistic, and it highlights how Nietzsche, even in his efforts to affirm existence, sometimes willfully idealized and smoothed over the warts to the point where his existence-affirmation was perfected enough, ecstatic enough, and comforting enough to be bearable. Nietzsche undoubtedly took a positive step towards a more earth-centered, existence-affirming standpoint, far beyond most of his contemporaries, but when the going sometimes got difficult, when the ugly details of existence presented themselves, he often became less of a participant in the sublime and awful Dionysian blood-soaked sacrifice, and more of a celebrant of the Apollonian deity, who requires that we see the unvarnished reality through a softening veil of beautiful idealization. When unadorned existence became nauseating, Nietzsche found solace in the beautifully dreamy Helen. In the above excerpt, Nietzsche's identification between reality itself and his woman-beloved, or alternatively described, between existential truth and his woman-beloved, only adds to the comforting way in which he characterized the world as a whole.

This is not to suggest that Nietzsche was weaker than most people in terms of his ability to face reality. He was probably supremely stronger than most, for he set forth and explored some of the most abysmal interpretations of the world that human beings can consider, and he often explored them fearlessly. One of these terrifying interpretations is the prospect of everything's utter meaninglessness and ultimate insignificance, where there is no intrinsic value, where the world is regarded as an accident and absurdity, and where everyone is fighting a losing battle against time and death. Few can come close to experiencing the reality that accompanies such a proposal's meaning, and among those who can see it clearly, most can usually contemplate it seriously for only a brief length of time. Even fewer people can live in practical accord with this idea for more than a day or two, and it is rare for anyone to develop an entire lifestyle in complete accord with such a thoroughly uninspiring and hopeless possibility.[153]

It is easy enough to talk about one's own death, or more grandly, about the possible extinction of humanity, but it is difficult to see the practical outcome of what such discussion entails. The deaths we read about in the newspapers, or even witness, are never our own deaths. Few experience the absolute disintegration of all personal meaning and hope, and emerge with a clear and healthy head. Nietzsche went far in showing what such abysmal ideas actually imply. He was, and remains, the tour guide of how our mundane world would appear under the most frightful interpretation, acting in a role comparable to that which Dante Alighieri (1265–1321), in his *The Divine Comedy*, assigned to the spirit of the Roman poet Virgil as his own fictional guide through the punishments of hell. In this respect, both Nietzsche and Dante are cousins to contemporary psychiatrists, who through their understanding of the human mind reveal to us the torments of insanity.

Side-by-side with such insights, much within Nietzsche's philosophy remains unrealistic, mythic, idealized, hopeful, future-projective, and prescriptive. There is much that is not down-to-earth, insofar as it fails to represent a satisfaction with existence just as it happens to be. To appreciate further this tension within Nietzsche's outlook, it is useful to consider a straightforwardly logical matter: how judgments concerning the imperfection of the existing world can transform into judgments concerning the perfection of the existing world, once one's existence-affirming attitude is strengthened.

To interpret the world in terms of idealizations, or of perfected images formed by extrapolating from the shapes and conditions of actually-existing things, is to draw a difference between what is, and what ought to be, or what might be. A tree with a broken branch does not embody the perfect tree, just as a person with a noticeably weak will or a feeble intellect does not embody the ideal of willpower and strong intelligence. In such instances, one is typically disposed to say that the condition is not perfect. And the more idealizing one becomes, the more unrealistic one can become, the more disappointed with actual existence one can become, and the more intense one's longing for another world might thereby be. Extreme idealization removes a person imaginatively altogether from time and space, to the realm of the perfect circle, perfect love, and perfect wisdom – all of which can never exist on earth, precisely because they are perfect, godlike, shining ideals. The idealizing, perfecting mentality is not fundamentally existence-affirming, because in contrast to the imagined ideal type, existence always comes up short. When raw existence is contrasted with ideal types, it does not present itself as a good representative of the truth. This was exactly Plato's attitude towards physical existence, and we can understand why Nietzsche was not strongly attracted to Plato's philosophy, much as he respected his intellectual powers.

To interpret the actual world as a more perfect world, one must reduce the gap between what actually is and what ideally ought to be. Taking the logic a step further, to regard the present world as an absolutely perfect world, one must deny any distinction between what is and what ought to be. Such a closure would require resisting idealizations and imaginative projections that define what ought to be in a way that establishes a reality different from what can, in principle, actually happen, and which stands as a perfected backdrop against which one would estimate the value of what right now happens to be the case. Closing the gap between what is and what ought to be entails that we resist our desire to want infinitely more than what is within the scope of real possibility. For only when "what is" and "what ought to be" coincide can the existing world present itself as being a perfect world.

Within the sphere of realistic possibilities, there are two ways to bring "what is" and "what ought to be" into coincidence. The first is the standard way, which is to reform the existing world so that it more closely matches our ideal types. Examples of this strategy abound, such as when we exercise to shape our bodies into some pre-determined set of proportions, or when we simply act according to some plan. The second way, which is less common, is to reform our ideals so that they match more closely what already is. At the extreme of this strategy, one could say that for anything that is, "it does not get any better than this," for the ideal would be defined in coincidence with what already happens to be.

In Nietzsche's more existence-affirming moments, he urges us to identify fundamentally with this second strategy. It is the attitude of *amor fati*, or the love of fate; it is a completely accepting attitude that harbors no regret, no frustration, no disappointment, no hatred, and no discontent with the world as a whole, either as it was or as it will be, no matter what happens. To be able to live joyously, "no matter what happens," is Nietzsche's aim. His ideal is to have no ideals which devalue the way things are.

Within an attitude of unqualified existential affirmation, what was previously interpreted to be an imperfect world becomes a perfect world. What was previously seen as a repulsive hell – the world of murder, violence, betrayal, and disease – becomes a perfect environment, and thus becomes heaven. Through a reinterpretation of this sort, Nietzsche exalts the daily world and regards it as a heavenly world, insofar as he judges it to be a perfect world where what is, exactly matches what ought to be. For Nietzsche, as for many philosophers, existence is a perfection.[154] Within this attitude of complete existential affirmation, the daily world becomes – as the philosopher Gottfried Wilhelm Leibniz (1646–1716) maintained, although for very different reasons – the best of all possible worlds. Nietzsche expressed the underlying sentiment as follows:

> "*The world is perfect*" – so says the instinct of the most spiritual, most affirmative instinct –: "imperfection, the '*below* us' of every kind,

distance, the pathos of distance – even the absolute outcast belongs to this perfection." The most spiritual people, as the *strongest*, find their good fortune where others would find their demise.[155]

Such a heavenly daily world is not available for everyone to experience, for only those who have the strength to say "yes" to blood-curdling horror – only those who are strong enough to accept the world just as it is, with all of its repulsive aspects, as it has been, and as it will be, however it may be – will have this divine experience of the world. Nietzsche reserved the keys to this heaven for only the extremely strong-minded. Weaker people are condemned to live in a daily hell because their idealizations draw them into experiencing a frustrating world that fails, almost by definition, to meet their expectations; the strongest-minded people live in heaven, because they accept the world as it is. Within Nietzsche's outlook, as we have earlier noted, heaven and hell are the same place, namely, the daily world. The difference is only a matter of interpretation. Redemption becomes a matter of using one's interpretive strength to adopt a healthy perspective.

In psychoanalytic terms, Nietzsche's particular style of interpretative adaptation expresses what Freud called the "reality principle" – the principle whereby one achieves satisfaction by accommodating oneself to the realities of the outside world, as opposed to resisting them. Any resistance to, or any striving to transform, any of the world's particular conditions is to be done upon the strong background of one's fundamental acceptance of the world. In aesthetic terms, Nietzsche's prescription for redemptive reinterpretation calls upon one to regard each moment as embodying the perfection of a work of art. Such is one salient dimension of Nietzsche's "aesthetic justification" for existence.[156]

It might appear that Nietzsche advocated the satisfaction of all one's desires for improvement by tempering or eliminating such desires altogether, much as Schopenhauer prescribed. Such a strategy is also suggested by Buddhism, since Buddhists believe that suffering is caused by an excess of desire. If one eliminates the desire that the world should become a better place, so the thought goes, then one will become satisfied with the world as it is. Interestingly enough, the weight of Nietzsche's view runs contrary to this Buddhist idea, for he also believed that a flourishing condition requires an attitude that respects and desires change, challenge, drive, expansion, and conflict. So his more complicated position is that one should make great attempts to flourish, but do so with a realistic and courageous recognition of life's ills, along with the pains that such attempts will entail. Nietzsche did not recommend an escape from suffering, and urged us to grow well within the context of a troubling and troubled world. We should aim to grow and flourish with the sharp recognition that when winter sets in – and it can set in suddenly, at any given moment – one will perish. That the lilies and roses might be infected by insects, or that they might be quickly clipped by a pair of scissors, or that they will eventually die in any case, does not undermine their tendency to live naturally to their maximum. The inherent presence of transformation and death in all finite things does not depress them, and Nietzsche urged us to tap into the same kind of invigorating life energies that run through us.

Nietzsche's ideal of healthy living presents a kind of care-free living, which in the human case translates into a kind of dancing, joyful, playful, frolicking wisdom, coexisting side-by-side with the self-conscious awareness of one's upcoming death. His outlook combines intense optimism with the most severe realism. His ideal is one of sagacity tempered with naïveté.

The aesthetic justifications of life and existence

Since Nietzsche was an atheist, it might seem out of place to introduce the concept of "redemption" into a discussion of his philosophy, but this theme recurs throughout his work.[157] Within the history of Judaism and Christianity, "being redeemed" is linked with a payment to someone, either because a debt is owed, or because something is to be bought back, as in making a ransom payment. The crucifixion, for instance, is often understood to be an absolute payment to God for people's sins, and therefore, as an act of redemption. If someone is referred to as a "redeemer" within the Christian context, the suggestion is that the person is a Christ-figure of some kind – someone who, given their overflowing power, goodness, or other beneficial quality, is so rich that they can pay off an infinite debt.

More abstractly considered, if a certain idea is judged to have a redeeming value, it is thought of as having the power to save a person from what would otherwise have been an undesirable condition. In common parlance, a socially-offensive work of art is considered to have "redeeming value," insofar as this added value has the power to "buy back" the work from a condition of censure. The logic of redemption requires that whatever is to be "redeemed" stands in a condition of lack. Redemption consequently involves the satisfaction of a lack, or the balancing of a disproportionate situation. This links redemption to the idea of justice. If the cosmos is such that eternal justice is non-existent, then it would seem that religious redemption would be a nonsensical enterprise.

As early as 1872 in *The Birth of Tragedy*, Nietzsche expressed an ambivalence towards traditional moral values, even though he was not yet explicitly attacking them in a vociferous and concentrated manner.[158] This is observable in his effort to formulate a justification for the existence of the world that is "aesthetic," rather than "moral," and which is opposed to what had been done traditionally in connection with the problem of evil. Nietzsche himself discovered the contrasting pair of "aesthetic" vs. "moral" visions of the world in the early Greek philosophers, associating the moral vision with Anaximander (*c.* 540 BC) – in relation to whom Nietzsche could note affinities to Schopenhauer's views – and the aesthetic vision with Heraclitus (535–475 BC), who among the early Greek philosophers is arguably the key inspirational figure for Nietzsche.

Within a more recent setting, many thinkers prior to Nietzsche offered "theodicies" or "justifications of God's ways to humans" which intended to account for the evil in the world, and Nietzsche engaged in the same spiritual project, albeit within a framework that did not allow any direct appeal to an all-good, all-knowing, all-powerful being.[159] Avoiding the formulation of a theodicy within a Christian framework, he attempted to develop a justification for existence within a Greek framework, attending to some of the early Greek philosophical views in conjunction with the aesthetic experience of Greek tragedy. And as noted above, Nietzsche associated the contemporary German music of his time, especially in the figure of Richard Wagner, as having a redeeming quality: the world Nietzsche lived in would be justi-fied if there were to be a resurrection of cultural health. Wagner was the potential redeemer of European culture in Nietzsche's earlier view.

Nietzsche soon left Wagner's entourage, but he continued in his final years to recognize that redemption was one of Wagner's central themes: "The problem of redemption is itself a venerable problem. There is nothing about which Wagner thought more deeply, than the problem of redemption: his opera is the opera of redemption. With him, someone or other wants to be redeemed, here it's a little man, there it's a little young lady – this is *his* problem."[160]

Redemption was also Nietzsche's problem, but Nietzsche found Wagner's style of redemption to be objectionably Christian, decadent, life-denying, Schopenhauerian, and Buddhistic, which is to say that he found Wagner's style to be unrealistic and weak-minded. When the pains of the world are items from which one seeks escape, one tends to idealize and hope for a better world, located outside of the moment one happens to be in. He charged Wagner with this kind of escapism.

Nietzsche fought for a way to interpret the world that was stronger, more inspiring, and yet realistic, and he found it in what he referred to as an "aesthetic" justification for the world's condition. The source of this outlook resides within Nietzsche's interpretation of Heraclitus, within which Heraclitus is presented as having considered the world to be a morally innocent place. On the contrasting Christian view, the world is said to be the creation of an intellectually mature and self-aware being called "God," wherein whatever happens in the world can be given a determinate, intended meaning and moral import, because God is conceived of as all-good, all-knowing, all-powerful, and as, in effect, the Chief Justice and Supreme Auditor of the universe's moral accounts.

Nietzsche's Heraclitus saw the universe as ruled by a different kind of principle, less akin to a mature, all-knowing, morally-responsible adult, and more like an innocent, polymorphously interested, morally naïve, playful child. Here, where moralistic calculations remain at a minimum, trickster-like whimsicality, fun, and creativity are strong, and the "drive for play" is characteristic. What is "aesthetic" about this interpretation of the world-as-child's-play is its affinity to the creative, artistic mentality: the world is seen as an art-product of naïve creative forces, not unlike a sandcastle, which lasts only for a day, and only until the sands of time, along with the dissolving power of the ocean, wash it away into oblivion. The aesthetic justification of life and existence returns us to the naïve world outlook, where we become children once more, and where we make direct contact with the life energies that once flowed through us more powerfully:

> But say, my brothers, what is the child able to do, that even the lion cannot? For what must the predatory lion still become a child?

The child is guilt-free and forgetting, it is a new beginning, a
game, a self-rolling wheel, a first movement, a holy "Yes."

Indeed, for the game of creation, my brothers, a holy "Yes" is
needed: the spirit now wills *his* will, *his* world now redeems the
world of the one who had been lost.[161, 162]

What for some people amounts to regression, immaturity, irre-
sponsibility, immorality, and a rejection of all that is civilized, for
Nietzsche signifies a liberation from social constraint, stagnation,
oppression, rigidity, unimaginativeness, and guilt. The moral view
of the universe is determined by moral laws; the aesthetic view of
the universe is open-ended. The moral justification of the
universe requires an all-knowing, all-powerful, all-good God; the
aesthetic view of the universe requires the strength to believe that
the universe is innocent, as it spews out volcanic lava, disease, and
floods that burn and kill innocent children. Just as one does not
blame a child for pulling the legs off a spider in an act of curiosity,
one would not blame the universe for the torments it inflicts
upon children.

Operative in Nietzsche's proposal of an "aesthetic" justification of the world is the attempt for a relief from guilt. Within this
aesthetic perspective, the universe is conceived of as a being that
does not admit of any ascriptions of guilt, for it has no moral
intentions. Within this aesthetic perspective, it makes no sense to
say that the world, in reference to its intrinsic nature, is "unjust" or
"just." Like an innocent child, it acts naturally. Like an innocent
child, the universe giggles, laughs, and jokes, if it has any sentiments at all.

Nietzsche believes that adopting the view of the universe as
being akin to a naïve child is redemptive, since it is guilt-alleviat-
ing and morally liberating. Those living within Nietzsche's
surrounding culture did not seem to have been adopting this
view *en masse*, and he therefore hoped that such an attitude would
arise in a more healthy future. Nietzsche even formulated this

hope in messianic terms, referring to its advancement as his own personal task, as the task of his fictional character Zarathustra, and as also the task of an actual spiritual leader of the future – a kind of messiah – as defined by his idea of the superhuman who possessed superhuman health:

> Zarathustra once defines, quite strictly, his task – it is mine, too – and there is no mistaking his meaning: he says Yes to the point of justifying, of redeeming even all of the past.[163]

> Is this [great health] even possible at this time?… But sometime, in a stronger period than this rotten, self-doubting present is, he must come to us, a *redeeming* person of great love and contempt, the creative spirit, whose surging force always keeps him away from everything remote and beyond, whose solitude is misunderstood by the general population, as if it were an escape *from* reality – while it is only his sinking-into, burying-into, deepening *into* reality, so that, when he eventually comes back into the light, he can bring home the *redemption* of this reality: its redemption from the curse laid upon it by the ideal that has been prevailing until now. This person of the future, who will redeem us from both this prevailing ideal and that *which will grow out of it*, from the great disgust, from the will to nothingness, from nihilism, this bell-stroke of noon and the great decision which again frees the will, that gives back to the earth its goal, and gives back to people their hope, this Antichrist and antinihilist, this conqueror over God and nothing – *he must come some day*. [164]

A traditional Judeo–Christian dimension to Nietzsche's thought – if not a more specific millennialist one – is evident here.[165] In many of his visionary moments, Nietzsche is disposed to prophesy, and he waits for another, better, Christ-of-health – a figure which is Zarathustra-inspired, which is of this flesh-and-blood world, but which is nonetheless superhuman, just as Jesus was purported to be. When he philosophized along this avenue, Nietzsche remained discontented with the way the world happens to be, and he formed a distinct idea of how a better world would appear. In a distant way, Nietzsche shared the sentiments of the Jewish people as he awaited for his messiah, having not been satisfied with the spiritual message that Jesus conveyed. If one recognizes that Jesus was raised within Jewish culture and that his central recorded message – the Sermon on the Mount – offered a new, contemporary interpretation of the Ten Commandments of Jewish law, the affinities are further strengthened. Consider the following words by Nietzsche's Zarathustra, which clearly intend to revise Jesus' well-known Sermon on the Mount: [166]

> "Thou shalt not steal!" "Thou shalt not kill!" – people once held such words to be holy; one bent the knee and head before them, and took off one's shoes. But I ask you: where in the world have there been better thieves and killers, than in these holy words?
>
> Is there not present in all life – robbing and killing? And by calling such words holy, was not the *truth* itself thereby killed? Or was it a sermon of death that was called holy, which contradicted and spoke against all life? – O my brothers, break, break the old tablets! [167]

Such Zarathustrian reflections arise within the context of life-affirmation, where flourishing health is to be maximized and sickness is to be minimized. Ideally, if one were super-healthy, one would never be sick, and one would live indefinitely. Sickness minimization is tantamount to death-minimization. Total flourishing-affirmation is tantamount to total death-denial. This way of considering Nietzsche's view fits with his doctrine of eternal recurrence, for even though the doctrine precludes an escape into an imaginative world beyond, it does guarantee that one will recur, or be resurrected, forever. The doctrine guarantees, in other words, that one will never fully go out of existence in the very long run. So there is an element of death-denial built into the doctrine as Nietzsche tends to formulate it.

An existentially stronger version of the doctrine of eternal recurrence would replace Nietzsche's idea of eternal repetition and recycling in a series of exact reiterations, with the idea of affirming that things will always be different, and that nothing will ever be the same as it is now, even though what happens might not be any better than it is now. The elements of the world might be continuously recycled, but in a fashion where every new constellation will be iterated only once in eternity.[168] In this respect, Nietzsche's conception of life-affirmation as expressed in the doctrine of eternal recurrence does not embody the thought of one's absolute non-existence, because on this redemptive doctrine, as manifestly construed, one never dies absolutely.

The version of eternal recurrence as "the recurrence of what is always different," in contrast to "the exact recurrence of what has already happened," leads to an affirmation of one's life that more obviously recognizes its inherent finitude. One can even argue that the "recurrence of what is different," or more simply, the notion of "always being different," is a more realistic doctrine, although whether it would be equally redemptive is debatable. However one decides this question, Nietzsche does present us with an unconventional and existentially-grounded way to be "redeemed," namely, through his general interpretation of the world as the Will to Power, his interpretation of the ideal living condition in reference to the Superhuman Being, and his interpretation of the world in terms of the doctrine of Eternal Recurrence.

Just as "imperfection" makes sense only in reference to the idea of "perfection," the notion of "seeking redemption" makes sense only in reference to that of "achieving redemption." If one's condition were interpreted as lacking nothing, or as owing nothing, then redemption would not be needed. Anyone concerned with seeking redemption is, by definition, in a condition of dissatisfaction or lack. An existence-affirming person, alternatively, would regard the world as being perfect just as it is, and would not need redemption. An existence-affirming person would already be redeemed in having achieved a state of mind that is beyond good and evil, where guilt is no longer experienced.

Since it is coherent to seek redemption only when one is not speaking from the standpoint of existence-affirmation, Nietzsche's "redemption-related" discourse should be regarded as the Nietzsche who was "on the way" to a more healthy standpoint, as opposed to the Nietzsche who had already achieved it. To a large extent, Nietzsche's philosophy was written by someone who struggled for redemption, not unlike the way someone struggles to explain the presence of evil in the world. The following excerpt expresses this intermediate position: "The deep instinct for how one must *live*, in order to feel oneself 'in heaven,' to feel 'eternal,' while in every other behavior one feels plainly not 'in heaven': this alone is the psychological reality of 'redemption' – a new mode of life, *not* a new faith."[169]

In a more generous interpretation, Nietzsche's more predominant standpoint – that of life-affirmation, or health-affirmation, or flourishing-affirmation – places him in a position comparable to a Bodhisattva-like figure who, although capable of achieving ultimate enlightenment (here equated with existence-affirmation), remains by choice in a finite condition. Remaining as such, he speaks intentionally in finite terms and with benighted conceptual constructions, for the purposes of guiding people effectively along the path towards existence-affirmation.

In a less generous interpretation, Nietzsche never quite lived up to the ideal of existence-affirmation that he often set forth, and he concluded his intellectual life, consequently, as a "sinner" in comparison to the sunlight glory of his own gods of well-being, under whose wing every imaginable fortune counts as a good fortune, where nothing is either pathological or pathetic, and where even a tragic crucifixion is transformed into a thrilling dance with fate. Such was Nietzsche's joyful wisdom that flowed from his aesthetic vision of existence. It is a world-interpretation within which events such as the crucifixion transform from a tragedy in the moral sense to a tragedy in the theatrical sense. It is a world-interpretation within which all the world becomes a stage, where every story carries the intrinsic value of its own play, but where the story remains a tale told by an idiot, or by a sand-castle-building child, signifying nothing in the grand scheme of things. It is also a world-interpretation within which one strives to use one's willpower redemptively, by trying to transform every pain into a birth-pang. In this way, one justifies the existence of pain by first noting how it defines a point of limitation for one's activity, and then acting to overcome it in an effort to create a stronger character for oneself, as if one were giving birth. In a large part, Nietzsche resolves the traditional problem of evil through the idea of willfully giving to one's original character a sublime and renewingly sublimated style.[170]

Had Nietzsche lived to witness the fate of his philosophical writings, he might have had his greatest interpretive challenge of all, since they were used to justify some of the worst atrocities ever committed by humans against their fellow humans. Nietzsche, though, had a dim glimpse of what his intellectual destiny might hold. At the end of his career, he wrote the following: "I know my lot. One day, my name will be remembered in connection with something awesome – a crisis like no other on earth, a most profound collision of conscience, a decision exorcised against everything to date, that has been believed, demanded, and made holy. I am no person; I am dynamite."[171]

Nietzsche had in mind for himself an association with a great enlightenment, a great revolution, a traumatic moment of cultural growth, and a period of world-crisis that would issue in a glorious rejuvenation of humanity. He hoped that his name would be linked to one of the finest renaissances of culture. As things now stand, his name remains linked with one of humanity's most depressing performances, given how long people have had to cultivate their caring sensibilities for each other. One truly hesitates to imagine the macabre fate Friedrich Nietzsche's writings would have had, had the Nazis won the Second World War.

7

The contemporary shadows of Nietzsche

Nietzsche and Nazism

When considering the links between Nietzscheanism and Nazism, one of the first images that comes to mind is the 1934 publicity photograph of Adolf Hitler gazing at the bust of Nietzsche during a visit to the Nietzsche Archives in Weimar. This guilt by association did not help Nietzsche's reputation outside Germany before the War, nor did it help his reputation virtually anywhere afterwards. Previous to the Nazi inhabitation of the Nietzsche Archives, and a stimulus to it, was Nietzsche's sister's social ingratiation with Benito Mussolini and Hitler in an effort to spread her brother's ideas to a wider population, and which in the long run, probably damaged as much as they promoted Nietzsche's overall popularity.[172] Academic study of Nietzsche's thought lagged during the post-Second World War era, needless to say, significantly on account of the Nazis' appropriation and linkage of his thought to their own anti-Semitic and nationalistic ideology.

Although some of Nietzsche's ideas can be interpreted as conforming with those of the Nazis, the differences between the two outlooks are more pronounced than the similarities, and it would be a mistake to understand Nietzsche's mature views as expressive of a strident, uncompromising, and aggressive German nationalism. The young Nietzsche who stood under Richard Wagner's fatherly wing unequivocally asserted that German culture would lead the way to a healthier Europe, but by the end of his career, Nietzsche was thoroughly disillusioned with Wagner and the "German spirit":

> Is Wagner a person at all? Is he not a sickness? Whatever he touches he makes sick – *he has made music sick.*[173]

> And so one understands the descent of the *German spirit* – from distressed intestines... The German spirit is an indigestion; it is never finished with anything. [174]

> I am such, that in my deepest instincts, I am alien to all that is German, so that even the proximity of a German inhibits my digestion...
> As far as Germany extends, it *spoils* culture. [175]

> The German spirit is *my* bad air: I find it hard to breathe in the vicinity of what has now become an instinctive uncleanliness *in psychologicis*, which every word, every facial expression of a German betrays.[176]

These anti-German, anti-nationalist, words are strong – at least in reference to the Germany Nietzsche observed during his lifetime – and one encounters Nietzsche enthusiasts citing them, fairly enough, in an effort to distance him from the Nazi nationalist doctrines that later surfaced. Indeed, Nietzsche's negative pronouncements on the German spirit might very well have led to his political execution had he been alive to give them public voice in Nazi Germany. Such defenders of Nietzsche accordingly aim to protect his view from association with the German government's mass murdering of Jewish, Gypsy, homosexual, infirm, mentally retarded, and other minority groups – crimes that were committed under Nazi rule several decades after his death. His attacks on anti-Semitism are also cited in his defense – attacks he directed towards his sister's husband, Bernhard Förster, and towards Richard Wagner, both of whom harbored hate for the Jewish people, and both of whom Nietzsche personally found upsetting.[177]

Nietzsche's infamous remarks about "the beast of prey, the splendid *blond beast*" – those barbarian peoples of centuries ago who roamed, plundered, and raped throughout northern Europe – are similarly downplayed as relatively insignificant slips on his part, given the generally sophisticated, refined, and generally humanly-sensitive tenor of his corpus. There remain a few "tough" interpreters of Nietzsche, but in the main, the "tender" Nietzsche has prevailed, with many mainstream Nietzsche scholars resisting, if only by means of remaining silent on the question, or by whitewashing the matter, acknowledgment of any substantial connection between Nietzsche and Nazism. The blame for this sinister association is, with some justification, usually placed squarely upon the shoulders of Nietzsche's sister, since he was either insane or already dead by the time his sister emerged within the public arena as his advertising agent.

As a consequence of such scholarly tendencies, readers of Nietzsche's works can be led quietly to believe that the connection between his ideas and those of the Nazis reduces to an unfortunate perversion of his true outlook, much like the Crusades and Spanish Inquisition can be regarded as transgressions of the Christian spirit of peace and love, as they stand in contradiction with Jesus' spiritual message. There is some truth in this comparison, but the doctrinal and historical affinities between Nietzscheanism and Nazism are not non-existent.

With respect to theoretical inspiration for National Socialism itself, one of the leading figures in the background to Nazi thought is the Englishman, Houston Stewart Chamberlain (1855–1927) – a writer eleven years Nietzsche's junior who grew up in France, became an ardent Germanophile, and later married Richard Wagner's youngest daughter, Eva. Wagner's son-in-law was the author of *Foundations of the Nineteenth Century* (1899), a lengthy anti-Semitic volume which elevated the Teutonic people over the Jewish people, promoting the former as the future leaders of Europe, while prejudicially condemning the latter.[178] The book is difficult to locate these days, and it has largely been passed over in silence by contemporary scholars who specialize in Nietzsche's twentieth-century legacy in Germany, as if its ideas are too outrageous and intellectually shoddy to merit serious scholarly attention. From exclusively moral and critical-scholarly perspectives, the neglect is defensible.

The historical fact, though, is that Chamberlain's anti-Semitic volume was immensely popular in Germany, selling strongly during the First World War, and continuing with sales in the hundreds of thousands by 1938. From the standpoint of under-standing German and European cultural history, Chamberlain's work cannot be ignored, as distasteful as some might find the proper examination of his thought to be. While Chamberlain's book enjoyed widespread publication, Nietzsche's *Thus Spoke Zarathustra* fared even better: during the First World War, the German government issued to its soldiers, for inspiration, Nietzsche's *Zarathustra* along with the Bible. In terms of their comparative popularity in Germany, these two books were both on the best-seller list, so to speak, within the same country, and within the same population.

It is also a remarkable curiosity that Houston Stewart Chamberlain assumed the role within the Wagner family circle that Friedrich Nietzsche once enjoyed, adoring Richard Wagner as an inspiration, and developing a deep attachment to Wagner's wife, Cosima – a person towards whom Nietzsche had himself expressed feelings of endearment. Nietzsche's relationship with Wagner ended in the late 1870s; Chamberlain's interest in Wagnerian opera began only a few years later, in the early 1880s, immediately before Wagner's death in 1883. In 1888, Chamberlain met Cosima Wagner, and soon thereafter entered into the Wagnerian "inner circle" – a circle whose leadership had been assumed by Cosima, who in due time came to regard Chamberlain much as she would a son.[179]

Most consequentially, Chamberlain, who eventually became a well-known German nationalist and anti-Semite, met with the young Adolf Hitler during the 1920s, and having been thoroughly impressed with Hitler's nationalistic enthusiasm and oratory talents, called upon him to be the future savior of Germany. Had Nietzsche not collapsed in 1888 – the year when Chamberlain began to assume a role in the Wagner family circle analogous to that which Nietzsche once had – he would have been linked with Hitler via Chamberlain's friendship with the Wagners, for at that late date, Nietzsche still harbored some strong affections for Cosima.[180] All in all, it seems that in view of historical considerations, Nietzsche never completely escaped from the Wagners' spiritual grasp: although he officially disengaged himself from the Wagner circle in the late 1870s and remained ambivalent thereafter, his work later fell back into association with this Wagnerian, anti-Semitic circle after he lost the ability to speak for himself.

Appreciating the manifest discontinuities between Nazism and Nietzscheanism is not difficult. Nietzsche, for one, was not overtly anti-Semitic, and most of the negative remarks he made about the Jewish people are counterbalanced by positive judgments.[181] During his intellectual prime, his attitude towards the Jewish people was nuanced and complicated: depending upon the subject and the context, his judgments varied. Nietzsche was inspired by many Old Testament personages, but he also realized that the Christianity he hated had its beginnings with Jesus, who was Jewish. Neither was Nietzsche ardently nationalistic during the 1880s, as noted. And even though he was, in principle, sympathetic to warriors and military types, his conception of the warrior was more closely linked to idealized classical heroics, courage, and daring, rather than to any soldiers who consider it their mundane business to massacre unarmed civilians.

What is additionally revealing, however, and what is far less attractive with respect to Nietzsche's position, is a consideration of the abstract format and rhetorical tone of many of his remarks, as they compare to what one typically finds in Nazi rhetoric. If we reconsider the comparison at this higher level of abstraction, some affinities emerge between Nietzscheanism and Nazism that are not readily noticeable when one remains content to cite their manifest doctrinal differences, of which there are sufficiently and significantly many. These discernible affinities obtain not only between Nietzscheanism and Nazism, but among a network of outlooks, all of which express characteristic "us vs. them" mentalities that set human beings against each other. If one considers the format and rhetorical tone of some of Nietzsche's remarks, especially during his last two years of intellectual activity, one can discern a conflictual, combative, self-glorifying, other-deprecating, and violence-affirming dimension that locates many of Nietzsche's views within a broad family of outlooks within which one can include Nazism.

It is important to qualify the above claim by noting that what is being considered here is a salient, but not thematically exhaustive, aspect of Nietzsche's thought. The Nietzschean philosophy is a prismatic, multidimensional, and complicated outlook, or more accurately, a set of outlooks in mutual tension, and it is a well-known problem that quotations can be ushered in to defend a variety of incompatible outlooks all counted as "Nietzsche's outlook." The Friedrich Nietzsche now under consideration is the "flourishing-affirming" rather than "existence-affirming" Nietzsche. Flourishing-affirmation is central to his intellectual stance, but it is arguably not the best perspective Nietzsche had to offer, since the existence-affirming perspective is more tolerant, more accepting, less aggressive, and probably more healthy, given the high, often self-destructive, pitch at which people's animalistic and aggressive energies can be exerted. Nietzsche's hard-line conception of flourishing might have been too extreme, if only because peacefulness and flourishing might be less antagonistic to one another than he supposed.

A straightforward way to consider the affinity between Nietzscheanism and Nazism is to recall Hitler's antagonism towards the Jewish people that he expressed in print[182], and compare this to what Nietzsche said about groups – albeit different groups – which he himself deprecated. It is disheartening to discover a comparably intolerant, condemning, and biting mind. Nietzsche's remarks cited above about the Germans being responsible for "ruining" European culture wherever they go rhetorically match Hitler's remarks about how the Jewish people had supposedly degraded, poisoned, corrupted, and undermined the health of German culture.[183] Neither are the comments by Nietzsche cited above isolated instances, and they became more caustic as he drew closer to the end of his career.

Nietzsche's description of priests, particularly Christian priests (such as his father), for instance, as "the most dangerous kind of parasite, the real poison-spider of life" is typical.[184] [185] Similar also are Nietzsche's claims that St. Paul was a "hate-inspired counterfeiter,"[186] that the principle that all people are equal stands against "all that is noble, gay, high-minded on earth,"[187] that the New Testament is so unclean that one needs to "put on gloves" when reading it,[188] that industrial culture in its present shape (of 1882) is "altogether the most vulgar form of existence that has yet existed,"[189] that those who teach resignation are so repulsive that he (through the character of Zarathustra) says, "to whatever is small and sick and scabby, they crawl like lice; and only my nausea prevents me from crushing them,"[190] that the priestly, ascetic ideal has ruined European spiritual health more than either alcoholism and syphilis,[191] and many other remarks that complain of European culture being polluted, sickened, weakened by particular kinds of people and belief systems, usually associated with the idea of, and the morality characteristic of, an all-powerful, all-good, all-knowing God.

Sometimes when reading Nietzsche, one feels that in his worst moments, the psychological venom with which he attacked Christians was comparable to the venom with which Hitler attacked the Jewish people. It is from the same bottle of poison that rabid racists attack those who are unlike them, and religious fanatics attack those who stand opposed to their doctrinal expansion. As expressed in the relatively small number of Nietzsche's most foaming-at-the-mouth passages, there is an anti-Christian mentality that is temperamentally foreign to neither the Nazi mentality, nor to extreme racist, religious, and nationalistic fanaticism: representatives of such views often call from the rooftops that the surrounding culture is becoming "polluted," that the situation is "now" at a crisis level, and that something radical needs to be done, lest disaster be the consequence. Among anti-Christians, anti-Semites, racists, and religious fanatics alike, subgroups engage in hate-speech directed at the supposedly polluting population, although there are always differences of opinion regarding who, exactly, is responsible for the cultural degeneration, and how this pollution is to be remedied.

Nietzsche, much to his credit, mostly advocated comparatively peaceful solutions that involved modifications in belief-systems, combined with a self-improvement program based on enhanced personal strength and greater aesthetic discrimination; Hitler dealt with his perceived situation as if he were battling a plague.[192] Nietzsche, in his best moments, tended to regard his surrounding culture with the high-minded, elitist sensitivity of an aristocratic and cultured physician; Hitler, on the other hand, formulated ruthless and brutal solutions that proved themselves to be self-defeating and inhuman. Both were, however, concerned generally with the same problem, namely, that of how to foster a spiritually healthy culture, either broadly conceived as the culture of the human species, or narrowly conceived as the exclusive health of a special subgroup of people. For better or worse, they both made themselves out to be cultural physicians.

When conceived in these abstract terms, a philosophical and practical question presents itself regarding the degree of violence that is, in principle, and in specific situations, required to develop and maintain social strength and individual health. Nietzsche (in a number of remarks) and Hitler were on the side of those who believe that unless people have an opposing group to look down upon and to define themselves against – a common enemy or common "other" – then they will grow weak. Buddha and Jesus were of a different mind, as preachers of universal non-violence. Nietzsche (in other remarks) sometimes more reflectively suggested that the violence and "looking down" necessary to developing and maintaining one's health should be directed mainly against oneself, and not against others, so that one can grow beyond one's former perspective in terms of the way one interprets the world. Also, Nietzsche's existence-affirming perspective does not obviously require as much violence as does his flourishing-affirming perspective.

If the rhetorical affinity between Nietzsche's caustic remarks against Christians and Germans and the Nazis' anti-Semitism is recognized, there remains another aspect of Nietzsche's views that draws him miles apart from the Nazi mentality. Moreover, one can argue that this aspect is stronger and more healthy than that through which Nietzscheanism and Nazism can be regarded as members of a loose-knit conceptual family. To appreciate this difference, it is first worth recalling once more a fundamental theme of Nietzsche's thought, namely, that of "health vs. sickness." As a philosopher of life-affirmation, the categories of "health" and "sickness" come to the foreground, often taking precedence over the distinction between "truth vs. falsity" and "pain vs. pleasure." Here, if lies and pain can serve the interests of health, then lies and pain acquire a positive value; if truth and pleasure run contrary to the interests of health, then they acquire a negative value. Health is the pivotal value in Nietzsche's thought, and traditional moral values take a back seat.

When philosophizing in terms of health, one is led quickly to interpret the world using terms such as "disease" and "sickness." When philosophizing in reference to social health, one naturally turns one's attention to those social forces that suggest themselves as counter-productive and threatening to the social order. In some societies, the status quo persecutes the unemployed; in others, it persecutes the insane; in still others, it persecutes minority ethnic or religious groups. Whatever the group happens to be, their social deprecation often issues from a mentality that considers social organizations to be living organisms, and that acts like a doctor who identifies social ills and their likely remedy. So once Nietzsche set his thought along the path of "health vs. sickness," and once he started to regard himself as a cultural physician, it was inevitable that he would identify certain aspects of the social order as undesirable, and as the causes of social disease.

This train of thought arises in most social theories – certain optimal social conditions are imagined and the present society is measured up against the proposed standard. What is at issue in Nietzsche's philosophy in connection with the Nazis is the degree of violence and repression that his philosophy can be taken to prescribe or condone. According to Nietzsche, life – and he seems to be quite right here – involves some degree of competition and violence, and we must ask how much violence is necessary for health, given that some is unavoidable. Although one might be required to kill other living beings for food, circumstances still might allow one to choose to be either a herbivore or a carnivore or an omnivore. Comparable choices apply at the level of human communities in interaction. Sometimes drastic measures are needed to direct the society towards a desired end; sometimes they are not needed.

So if one's body or community is under a threat of death, then one might be able to justify actions that intend to destroy the threat. If one's body or community is in a weakened condition, then the threat will increase proportionally. If one's body or community is in a strong condition, then the threat will decrease proportionally. At the maximum, if one were invulnerable, then one could not be threatened, and would be in a position to live peacefully with forces that would kill other, weaker types. Neither would the concepts of danger or fear make sense to such an invulnerable being. An absolute defense would amount to an absolute offense.

Given this logic, Nazism can be seen as the doctrine of a psychologically weakened and defensive society that felt threatened and vulnerable, for the rulers of that society saw the need to protect themselves and their followers by attempting to annihilate a perceived mortal threat. War and aggression, in other words, need not be expressions of strength, and can just as easily be expressions of fear and vulnerability. In some of Nietzsche's reflections, he perceived this kind of aggression as the expression of weakness, and he aspired to a different kind of strength – one where one is so strong that even poisoned waters cannot undermine one's health. This is a strength that can find a source of enjoyment in misery, that does not turn away from pain, and does not simply survive, but says "yes" to tragic life-episodes that would ordinarily be crushing. Such a person would not need to use violence as a defense, nor would such a person experience much hate. Nietzsche expressed such general ideas in *Thus Spoke Zarathustra*:

> When among people, whoever does not want to die of thirst, must learn how to drink from every glass; and whoever among people wants to remain clean, must know how to wash even with contaminated water.[193]
>
> And so I spoke to myself in consolation, "Well now, take courage old heart! A misfortune made things go wrong – savor that as your good fortune!"[194]

> Indeed, the human being is a contaminated river. To be able to absorb a contaminated river, without becoming unclean, one must already be an ocean. Look, I teach you the superhuman: he is this ocean; in him your great contempt can descend.[195]

Note, in contrast, the relative weak-mindedness that shows itself to be characteristic of the noble type which Nietzsche describes in the following canonical quote, also written when he was at the height of his career. This noble, or "master," type still looks down on others, and still feels contempt for those who are more vulnerable:

> Despised are the cowardly, the apprehensive, the petty, those who are concerned merely with narrow utility; also the suspicious ones with their constrained look, those who lower themselves, the doglike types, who allow themselves to be mistreated, the begging fawners, the liars above all – it is a basic belief of all aristocrats, that the common folk are untruthful. "We who are truthful" – that is what the nobility in ancient Greece called themselves.[196]

The point suggested here is that some of Nietzsche's characterizations of the noble, strong, or "master" type appear to have been written from a condition of less-than-perfect health and less-than-optimal strength. Despite this, there were occasions when Nietzsche realized that if one is super-healthy, and if one is thoroughly flourishing, then there is no need to project negative attitudes on other, less healthy, people – one could be so strong as not even to be bothered by a supposedly disintegrating culture. This would be the extreme limit of such an attitude – one where, culturally speaking, in one's "loneliest of loneliness," one could still say "yes" to the culture, even though it might be in a questionable spiritual state. As Nietzsche said himself, it would be a condition where one could say "yes" to the world wholeheartedly, desiring that nothing should be changed, even those people whom one believed, truly or falsely, to be undermining the culture.

If one takes to their limit a salient cluster of Nietzsche's remarks on what counts as a healthy attitude towards life, one would be directed to become the opposite of the generally "Nazi" types, whose views are marked by discontent with the national or cultural condition, and whose fear for the health of the nation or culture reaches levels of absolute intolerance towards those who do not share their conception of health. In contrast to this mentality, a healthier person would accept the cultural situation as it is, and discover ways to flourish within it, with all of its perceived imperfections, however these are defined. This would display an even greater strength. From the outside, it might appear that one was "turning one's other cheek" to the perceived threat, and behaving in a distinctively Christian way; from the inside, it would be that one was in fact so strong that the threat was nothing difficult to digest:

> A stronger and more well-turned-out person digests his experiences (his ordinary actions and criminal actions included), as he digests his meals, even when he has to swallow some hard mouthfuls. If for some experience, he cannot "be done with it," this kind of indigestion is as much physiological as the other – and in fact, it is frequently only a result of the other.[197]

Nietzsche and twentieth-century French philosophy

As noted above, after his early retirement from the University of Basel at the age of thirty-four, Nietzsche spent the remainder of his intellectually active life moving gypsy-like from place to place. His center of gravity was in the Swiss Alps, and his travels extended to the sea and riverside towns of Italy, with a return north to Germany in most years to visit his mother. At this point in his life, Nietzsche developed into a more cosmopolitan thinker, and as his identification with southern Europe increased, his

German nationalism diminished. Although Nietzsche was raised in Germany and wrote in the German language, he is not a proto-typical "German philosopher," for many of the cultures and ideas which inspired him – first and foremost ancient Greece – were located outside Germany. Much like the Jewish people had lived for centuries, Nietzsche had no proper homeland during the prime of his life, living in the places he stayed as much of an alien as he was a citizen.[198] If there was any culture that he tended to favor wholeheartedly, it was the French culture, even though he did not, strangely enough, travel extensively in France: "Fundamentally, it is a small number of old Frenchmen to whom I repeatedly return: I believe only in cultivation as it is understood by the French, and hold everything else in Europe that calls itself 'cultivated,' to be a misunderstanding, not to mention German culture."[199 200]

As was true of Nietzsche's intellectual reception in the English-speaking countries, his reception in France during the twentieth century was initially sluggish. He was also less attractive to academic philosophers, and had a more noticeable following among writers and avant-garde artists. Just as Schopenhauer became a philosopher for musicians during the later nineteenth century, Nietzsche became a philosopher for writers and poets during the early twentieth. Although the surrealistic movement of the 1920s directly owes much to Sigmund Freud's influence, it was Nietzsche who led the way in his extended attention to the unconscious, often unspeakable, sexually-centered, instinctual "Dionysian" forces within people. Freud was not the first to assert that the core truth of the human psyche is to be explained mainly in terms of our instinctual energies.

Georges Bataille (1897–1962), writer and philosopher, used the "acephalic man" (headless man) as his hallmark, combining in a single image the guillotine bloodbaths of the anti-aristocratic French Revolution, the idea of disempowerment through castration, and Nietzsche's anti-authoritarian call to remove the very "head" of reality, namely, God.[201] Nietzsche's affirmation of life impressed Bataille with its full Dionysian flavor, and Bataille observed that life not only requires violence and killing, but also requires the production of waste products. Since living things necessarily generate waste, Bataille concluded that perfectly balanced, equilibrium-centered, self-contained, recycling, and stabilized systems run counter to what was for him, the excretory and excremental nature of life itself. Balanced accounting sheets contradict the style of life's economy, because life always produces leftovers. Bataille consequently presented us with a Nietzschean philosophic vision that, imagistically-centered in the profusion of waste, accentuated Dionysian excess, superfluousness, expenditure, ecstasy, and overflowing rather than an Apollonian efficiency, controlled, perfected, rationalized, and tightly retained.

Within twentieth-century French philosophic thought, Nietzsche's stress upon aesthetics and wisdom was adopted enthusiastically, and achieved further expression in the uniquely French existentialist manner. In the mid-century, Jean-Paul Sartre (1905–80), existentialist philosopher and designate for the 1964 Nobel Prize for Literature (which he declined), developed his philosophical position by attending closely to the aesthetic texture of our day-to-day lives, locating the abyss – one that Nietzsche had once discerned in the meaningless chaos behind the apparently stable world – in a more obvious place. For Sartre, the upsetting aspect of the world is the reality of our day-to-day existence. It is the world of excretory products such as mucus, ear wax, phlegm, pus, bad breath, dandruff, vomit, scabs, urine, feces, dirty linens, small-minded bickering, petty betrayals, disillusionments, dried blood, bloated corpses, and buzzing flies. It is the daily world where people are mugged and murdered for only a few dollars. Such is the existential furniture in Sartre's version of mundane reality – his version of the paralyzing Medusa's face –

that it is difficult to behold without repulsion, without excuses, and without comforting idealizations.[202] Overexposure to this harsh aspect of reality, as so many war stories illustrate, can turn a person's emotions into stone.

Although Sartre's abyss is aesthetically defined in reference to the repulsive quality of raw existence, the Sartrean experience of "existential nausea" stands as a form of wisdom, for it represents a necessary part of the truth of what it means to be alive. Shakespeare's Sonnet 130, cited above, expresses the same down-to-earth awareness as does Sartre, but with a far more loving and rationally-balanced temperament. The Sartrean awareness of existence, in contrast, was grounded in the frustrating recognition that the uniqueness of individual things defies one's strongest efforts to comprehend them fully. For Sartre, existing individuals are absurd, and even after one is dead, one's corpse remains annoyingly "in the way."

Albert Camus (1913–60), novelist and philosopher, grounded his philosophy on the same Sophoclean and Shakespearean questions as did Nietzsche: "Why live?" and "To be or not to be?" According to Camus, the problem of suicide is the one serious philosophical problem, and his answer to the question of whether life is, or is not, worth living, similarly fused aesthetics and wisdom in a Nietzschean manner: for life to be maximally meaningful, Camus believed that we should live every moment with the joyful exhilaration of a person who, having been just released from prison, inhales the fresh air, and feels the sunlight and ground below, as if it were the substance of heaven itself. The experience is aesthetic and ecstatic, and it is accompanied by the wisdom that in reference to such an aesthetic experience – an experience available to all, at every moment – life becomes infinitely valuable, and that one should struggle to live as long as possible. Here, if one adopts a certain perspective, all moments are the same and are equally precious.

Camus concluded that the best life is the one that lasts the longest, throughout which one loves whatever happens. He believed that once a person realizes the infinite value of each moment in aesthetic exhilaration, considerations of "better or worse" will dissolve, and life will become only a matter of quantity. Being awake the longest is the best if one develops a positive attitude towards existence. For Camus and Nietzsche, existence itself can be perfection. Although their basic conclusions were the same, the temperamental difference between them resided in Camus's more pronounced emphasis upon the utter absurdity and sharp awareness of the mechanical quality of daily life. Camus, for instance, upon looking at a person talking away wildly in a telephone booth, and in suddenly being struck by the "incomprehensible dumb show" of the person's gestures, would stop and wonder why the person even bothered to be alive.[203]

During the more socially turbulent and revolutionary times of the 1960s, Nietzsche's popularity in French academic circles increased, mainly due to the inspiration of his "death of God" idea. This provocative thought became philosophically attractive, owing to its rejection of a determinately specified, ultimate authority that defines the absolute truth. The "death of God" might not have directly expressed the French Revolutionary values of equality and fraternity, but it captured the idea of liberty well, even though it was a noticeably iconoclastic sort of liberty. Nietzsche's call for the death of all absolute authority confirmed the aims of social revolutionaries who protested against oppressive social conditions – conditions which were particularly offensive in how they presented themselves as the natural and best way to live. It also inspired philosophic-literary thinkers such as Roland Barthes (1915–80) and Jacques Derrida (1930–2004), who rejected the idea that in principle the meaning of a text is determinate, and is determined primarily by the text's author.

The personage of Nietzsche-as-iconoclast was especially inspirational to social reformers and critics who regarded the capitalist status quo as a system well worth overturning. Nietzsche himself disapproved of Communism as much as he disapproved of Christianity, owing to what he perceived as their shared unrealistic visions of social harmony, peace, and equality. Nonetheless, the anti-capitalist, Marxist sentiments that ran as an undercurrent within twentieth-century French culture remained loosely compatible with Nietzsche's iconoclasm.

Another attraction of Nietzsche's thought in postwar France was his historical approach to understanding social phenomena. In *Human, All-Too-Human*, he stated controversially: "Everything, though, has become; there are no eternal facts: just as much as there are no absolute truths. From now on, therefore, *historical philosophizing* is necessary, and with it, the virtue of modesty."[204] It is not to Nietzsche's intellectual credit that this remark suggests self-underminingly, and somewhat entertainingly, that it is an eternal truth that there are no eternal truths, but his intent is clear: most of what we believe to be natural, true, unshakable, stable, and thoroughly reliable in our world is not that way at all. Just as a sheet of glass appears to be a solid, when it is in fact a very slowly flowing liquid, our social institutions, our labels for common things, our self-definitions, our value systems, only appear to be written in stone, when in fact they are, as a rule, or quite significantly, written only into the seashore sand. They are subject to change, and they are for the most part arbitrary, definitely malleable, and intrinsically eroding forms, not unlike our physical bodies. Perhaps, then, although one cannot assert coherently that absolutely everything is changing, a Nietzschean would hold, minimally, that almost everything is changing, especially those things that one holds near and dear.[205]

The thought that our world is fundamentally marked by transition, fluctuation, transformation, and other effects of time's passing can be found in early Greek philosophy in the vision of Heraclitus. The same idea of a prevailing impermanence to the world is also at the core of Buddhism. In Nietzsche, and in later twentieth-century French philosophy, this proposition assumes the form of a strong emphasis on and sensitivity towards philosophizing in view of historical change – a standpoint whose roots can be traced to German philosophy of the late eighteenth and early ninteenth centuries in the writings of Johann Gottfried Herder (1744–1803) and G.W. F. Hegel (1770–1831).

Nietzsche developed his conception of historical philosophizing using background assumptions that were unlike those of his predecessors, many of whom conceived of historical change as the realization of a timeless, grand, moral plan of the world (where our historical progress ends in a perfect society and justice is finally done). Nietzsche, by contrast, considered social phenomena as mere happenings whose complicated and overlapping histories can be set within an array of diverse, often accidental, and typically natural and non-moral sources. Rather than regarding history as the materialization of a previously determined cosmic plan that issues from an intrinsically rational universe, Nietzsche considered history to be the human narrative construction of meanings from meaningless and innocent events, which is to say that in our world, global historical meaning is created only by us and is not discovered as the revelation of the intentions of a universal, godlike being whose existence precedes that of the human being, and whose infinitely knowing intentions determine human fate, one way or another. In contrast to his nineteenth-century predecessors such as Hegel and Marx, Nietzsche's historical philosophizing avoided grand historical projections.[206] This dissolution of historically overriding aims was even more pronounced in those twentieth-century French philosophers who were influenced by these Nietzschean ideas, such as Michel Foucault (1926–84), who, like Nietzsche, interpreted the world in terms of fluctuating power-constellations.

Nietzsche's style of historical philosophizing, owing to its social revolutionary import, was also inspirational in French feminist thought during the post-Second World War period. Nietzsche himself might have had sexist tendencies, but his style of historical philosophizing fits the social, political, and moral interests of those thinkers such as Luce Irigaray (1931–), who assert that men should not be privileged over women in reference to social benefits, the availability of leadership roles, employment status, and power in general. By considering the history of sexism using the Nietzschean–Foucaultian style of historical analysis, one can argue that the dominant role men have taken in most societies has been neither naturally preordained nor morally defensible, but has been a socially-constructed phenomenon that can be changed to everyone's overall benefit through concerted social activism and linguistic reflection.

Similarly, by tracing social phenomena back to their diverse roots using Michel Foucault's Nietzsche-inspired style of genealogical analysis – much like one would trace the history of a person through the details of their family tree – one can describe how the various definitions of the "outcast" and the "criminal" that different societies have adopted are not steadfast valuations, but temporary social constructions. It is common knowledge that what counts as criminal behavior in one culture is legal in another. Instead of concluding from this that some societies have value systems that are closer to the absolute truth, Foucault and Nietzsche suggest that there is no common, universal, natural valuation, with which all legalities ought to coincide. This measure of freedom and tolerance is admittedly too uncontrolled for strict partisans of the Enlightenment spirit, for it also implies that there are no "unalienable rights" and no universal good; for others, especially those who have suffered unjust oppression and who have been kept at an unfair disadvantage at the hands of a dominating society, such an iconoclastic position stands as a liberating breath of fresh air. Post-Second World War French thinkers tended to appreciate Nietzsche's emancipating thought in the latter, more radical manner.

Central to Nietzsche's reluctance to define any "absolutes" in social theory or elsewhere, is his observation that people experience the world through many different perspectives, and that living things in general also adopt many alternative perspectives on the world. It is an easy thought-experiment to consider how wildly different our daily world would look to us, had we the ability to see radio waves and x-rays in addition to light rays, or could hear the very high pitches that dogs can hear, or could smell food located miles and miles away, as can polar bears. As a matter of fancy, Nietzsche described some imaginative changes to the human condition, to illustrate how particularly set, and how noticeably arbitrary, our given orientation to the world happens to be. In the following excerpt, he imagined what it might be like if the human perceptual uptake were slowed down considerably, as is done in the making of a time-lapse photograph or time-lapse movie.

> If a person could make only 189 perceptions during the year, then the difference between day and night would completely fall away; the sun's path would appear as a shining arc in the sky, just as a glowing coal, when swung around, would look like a fiery circle; the vegetation would continually shoot up and then vanish again in a tearing hurry.[207]

Nietzsche's "perspectivism" – the thought that all knowledge is only knowledge gained within the frontiers of some presupposed background or other, and that those backgrounds are diverse – was inspirational for twentieth-century French philosophy, owing to its compatibility with the idea that networks of social values vary with time and place, and that no perspective is final, at least when referring to human beings and their cultural perspectives.

How, then, should one choose among perspectives, when several alternatives are available? This has been asked of Nietzsche and of his French followers in the twentieth century. Nietzsche usually considered the resolution of such questions to be a matter of taste, which makes the resolution a matter of judgment, discrimination, and sensitivity. He saw no easy answer to appeal to as a matter of rigid rule. It is possible to feed one's mind with information of all kinds, to adopt any of a number of perspectives, and Nietzsche believed that the kind of person one is, and in particular, the level of health one has, largely determines the perspectives one adopts. Making a choice among perspectives, or simply gravitating unconsciously or instinctively to one perspective or another, he believed, is a reflection of one's state of health – a state which is itself reflected in one's capacity for judgment and discrimination.[208]

A further way to explain Nietzsche's answer to the question, "how should one choose among perspectives?" is to point out that words for "knowledge," "wisdom," and "taste" are closely related in their linguistic origins, and that to be a wise person is to be someone who has a fine capacity for judgment. This capacity is related to the discriminating powers of someone who is a connoisseur of food – a person who has "good taste." A cluster of associated words reveals the connection. In French, "*connaitre*" means "to know," but there is also the word, "*connoisseur*," which refers to a person of good taste. In French, the word "*savoir*" also means "to know," as does the Spanish word, "*saber*." In English, we have the related word "savor," which refers to the act of tasting food carefully.

As a philologist, Nietzsche was aware of these etymological connections, and he added that "*sapiens*," as in "*homo sapiens*," which is usually understood to mean "that which knows," actually means "that which tastes." So "*homo sapiens*" has a meaning that resonates with "the man who has developed a sense of taste" or "the man who has the capacity for fine discrimination."[209] Having wisdom, then, entails having good taste, at least etymologically. Boorishness and crudity would be opposed to wisdom, so one would not expect wisdom to arise among those who identify with the least common denominator within society. Nietzsche's aristocratic elitism, his distinct preference for "higher types," and his continual emphasis on aesthetic matters of taste can in this way be traced to his understanding of the ancient meaning of wisdom. Accordingly, he urged us to be more discriminating, as far as our given powers will allow. Nietzsche's emphasis on aesthetics and discrimination, as it was combined with his disposition towards understanding the world in terms of its minute historical detail, was inspirational to French thought of the later twentieth century.

In broad description, Nietzsche influenced twentieth-century French thought in his taste-related conception of wisdom, his open-minded perspectivism, his down-to-earth emphasis on historical philosophizing, his fearless attempt to look into the abyss, and his iconoclastic, authority-rejecting conception of freedom, which was linked with the "death of God." French philosophers who transformed and accentuated these Nietzschean ideas include Georges Bataille, Jean-Paul Sartre, Albert Camus, Roland Barthes, Michel Foucault, Jacques Derrida, Luce Irigaray, and Gilles Deleuze. Near the very end of the twentieth century, Nietzsche's influence waned in France, as the concepts of equality and fraternity rose to greater prominence in social theorizing, and as Nietzsche's aristocratic attitudes were increasingly regarded as being antagonistic to the enduring democratic spirit of the French Revolution.

Conclusion: Nietzsche, the jester of metamorphosis

Fate drew the shades on Nietzsche's final decade of life with an ailment, probably either syphilis or a brain infection, that left him unable to write or communicate coherently. His tragic psychological downfall came on 3 January 1889, at the age of forty-four, when he collapsed in the Italian riverside city of Turin, never again to regain his mental health. After a short hospitalization in Basel, and a brief residence at a sanatorium in Jena, he lived out most of his remaining years in Naumburg with his mother, in the house he knew as a teenager. After his mother died in 1897, Elisabeth Nietzsche moved him and his collected papers to Weimar, where she and her brother lived until his death on 25 August 1900. Whether Nietzsche's gradually intensifying illness significantly affected the content of his 1888 writings will remain a topic of debate, but the popular images of the bedridden Nietzsche during his last years of life hardly reflect his stature as one of the most important intellectuals of the nineteenth century. Perhaps it would be more intellectually proper to remember him as he was during his prime, between the years of 1880 and 1887, from ages thirty-six to forty-three – those fertile times when he wrote *Daybreak*, *The Gay Science*, *Thus Spoke Zarathustra*, *Beyond Good and Evil,* and *On the Genealogy of Morals*. And, as has been suggested implicitly in the preceding chapters, one can take a further step by aligning Nietzsche with the spirit of romanticism, and so to regard his final year as his most philosophically avant-garde.

We have seen that Nietzsche's outlook began to change significantly around 1886, and it is arguable that despite the rhetorically-inflamed quality of his 1888 works, the insights expressed in these writings were among his most intriguing and philosophically revolutionary. With the dissolution of the distinction between appearance and reality, Nietzsche's theoretical travels appear to have attained a greater awakening, for he arrived at the more fully existentialist viewpoint he had been seeking during his entire career. When appreciated from this angle, Nietzsche's writings reach a point of culmination, where he was at his best when he was most frenzied, and where at the close of his philosophical life, he submitted his concluding statements to posterity, and pounded his hands on the piano keyboard in a crashing finale.

In his final months of sanity, Nietzsche summarized his outlook in the following remarks:

> Fundamentally, there are two negations that my term *immoralist* contains. On the one hand, I negate a type of person which has been valued as the highest kind to date, the *benevolent*, the *charitable*; on the other hand, I negate a kind of morality, which has ruled and has been valued as morality itself – the morality of *decadence*, or more blatantly stated, *Christian* morality... To me, the over-valuation of the good and the benevolent will, considered globally, is the consequence of *decadence*, as a symptom of weakness, as incompatible with an ascending and yes-saying life: negation *and extermination* are the conditions of saying Yes. [210]

> I know the pleasure in *extermination* to a point commensurate with my *power* to exterminate – in both I obey my Dionysian nature, which knows of no separation between doing No and saying Yes. I am the first *immoralist*: and with that, I am the *exterminator par excellence*. [211]

Here, Nietzsche portrays himself as the very spirit of change – as someone in good company with Eris,[212] with Shiva,[213] with abysmal and awesome chaos, with transforming fire, and with death as the herald of rebirth – all in the service of cultivating a more intense cultural and personal flourishing. For Nietzsche, unbridled instinct is life's fire, and he saw his philosophy as a kind of bellows that could reignite a culture whose instinctual forces had been dangerously weakened by all too benevolent values, and which had forgotten the healthy spirit of the playfully creative and daring Greeks. While gazing into the terrifying abyss, Nietzsche found the strength to dance. While kissing his beloved, he defiantly faced the maggots that were poised to consume their bodies. While gazing in rapture at the sunset and stars, he acknowledged life's icy dreads to their maximum. Nietzsche understood the daily world as a paradise of pandemonium, and took it upon himself to guide others along towards a realistic and yet healthy outlook.

Although Nietzsche's vision is at once terrifying, sublime, beautiful, and inspiring, he might have given Christianity too much credit for having impressed its ethics of non-violence on the standing population. According to him, almost two millennia of Christianity – along with rationalistic thinking, and along with the adherence to other-worldly hopes – have weakened the human race, allegedly because these views have too effectively curbed people's allegedly natural tendencies to be greedy, violent, exploitative, aggressive, and dominating. But we can so easily and uneasily ask: has the history of the Western world since the time of the ancient Greeks been lacking in selfishness, violence, and people looking down upon one another with a view towards exploitation? A philosophy that urges us to be more instinctual than we already are might relieve some pent-up frustration, but it might also release self-destructive bloodshed.

Some believe that Christianity has demonstrated its cultural strength because the Christian belief-system has endured for two thousand years, and Nietzsche – someone who beheld that belief-system as life-weakening in principle – can be regarded as a thinker who, at the other end of the spectrum, intended to counteract this two-millennia-long enfeebled condition. As a third option, one can argue that either Christianity has failed, or that it has yet to complete its mission, if only because the increasing dangers of over-population, food and energy depletions, pollution, and devastating military weaponry have made the world environment more desperate and potentially more violent than ever before.

Perhaps a day will come when Nietzschean "hardness" will be required among world leaders to keep human civilization from spinning out of control to the point of self-destruction. It could also be true that a tiny reduction in worldwide greed and selfish-ness, or a tiny increase in worldwide compassion, would increase global health. Even if it is metaphysically false, the Christian – and every other – ethics of benevolent non-violence might be presently the most healthy ethics to foster, before the cosmopoli-tan situation becomes too critical and traumatic for benevolent solutions to be effective.

Despite his questionable attack on Christianity and his proba-ble misdiagnosis of the reasons behind the world cultural crisis – at least if one considers what he could not have foreseen, such as the recent world population explosion, the existing nuclear weapons arsenals, and the growing capacity for genocidal biological warfare – Nietzsche's philosophy remains useful in its perpetuation of what is perhaps another myth, namely, that the universe is careless and valueless. People are not obviously thrown into the world as aliens from another dimension, and they are not "made" out of clay by any observable hand. They grow out of the world naturally. So humanity is intrinsic to the universe, as are all other existing beings. Believing nonetheless, as does Nietzsche, that human beings are the only intelligent beings in existence, does carry a psychological benefit: it allows us to break free of other-worldly cosmic-parent images, and to take responsibility for our own actions and face our difficulties squarely. Nietzsche was an atheist, but he could hardly have disagreed with the adage, "God helps those who help themselves." As was to become true of Jean-Paul Sartre's philosophy in the years to come, Nietzsche's thought stands as one of the greatest philosophies of self-reliance and freedom made supreme.

To stop relying immaturely on one's heavenly parents for help, while also recognizing one's common humanity, would define a virtuous mean between the vicious extremes of selfish individualism and slavish communal conformity. Nietzscheanism helps foster creative independence in the first instance; Christianity, as one among many other human-essence-respecting views, helps foster mutual respect in the second. Among the many Christianity-affiliated alternatives, and, although Nietzsche's taste would consider it to be both insufficiently poetic and too rationalistic, the Enlightenment religion of Deism – the religion of a different Golden Age now lost, and of men such as George Washington, Thomas Jefferson, and Benjamin Franklin – approximates this intermediate ideal, for it acknowledges Dionysian freedom of thought and the realities of the material world, while it respects a stabilizing and universal Apollonian reason.

If any general conclusion is to be drawn, one can say that Friedrich Nietzsche – a cultural fugitive and theorist of intellectual homelessness – was desperately in love with "life itself," and wrote his chilling philosophy in view of the hard fact that life does not always treat one sympathetically, and sometimes tears one apart, even if life is the object of one's unconditional love. Much of Nietzsche's philosophy explores the implications – biological, psychological, philosophical, religious, social, political – of loving unconditionally a world that allows one to experience intense joy, only on the condition that one also experience intense pain. In this atheistic, yet purgatorial, outlook, a cross is still carried to the point of redemption – a redemption where one becomes dancingly reunited with one's all-encompassing, but very worldly, parent, which in Nietzsche's case is mother nature. This redemption is a *danse macabre*, through which one, like a daredevil, like a jester, and like an explorer, makes one's peace with an inhospitable, changing, and violent world, after having recognized within oneself the feral call of the wild. To sanctify life and to be true to life, while resisting the temptations of satisfying fantasy, was Friedrich Nietzsche's consuming task.

Glossary

Aesthetic vs. Moral Justification: a distinction made in connection with the problem of evil. A "moral" justification of the existence of evil refers us to the goods that existing evil helps bring into being, or the further evils that existing evil prevents. An "aesthetic" justification of the existence of evil refers us to the valuable knowledge, insight, or creativity that the aesthetic experience of an evil-containing world can provide

Apollonian: that which is related to imagination and dreams; features of experience that, by means of idealization, perfection, rationalization, or beautification, make the world a more comforting place to be

Asceticism: a general attitude and practical approach towards life that involves reducing one's worldly, animal, or instinctual desires as much as possible

Dionysian: features of experience that are associated with instinct, strong life-forces, daredevilry, sexuality, and ecstasy

Eternal Recurrence: the doctrine that there is no other world than the one in which we presently live, and that within this world, whatever happens will continue to repeat itself over and over again, either specifically or thematically

Existentialism: the philosophical view that directs our attention to our here-and-now experience as the absolute foundation for all further reflection on the world

"Gay Science": Nietzsche's ideal attitude towards life, which involves a dancing, joyfully thrilling, or gay attitude, fused with a strong awareness of life's more difficult-to-behold realities

Genealogy: a style of intellectual analysis where the many strands of historical detail that feed into a subject matter are assembled; the goal of genealogical analysis is to show how the subject matter emerged from diverse antecedent historical strands of conditions

"Joyful Wisdom": *see* **"Gay Science"**

Master Morality: a general style of moral thinking that emphasizes self-sufficiency, self-generativity of values, self-legislation, and independence; according to Nietzsche, this style is typical of those who have strong life energies

Nachlass: the name used to refer to Nietzsche's notebooks and unpublished writings; literally "leftovers"

Nihilism: the view that the world, or existence, or life, is intrinsically worthless

Overman: *see **Übermensch***

Perspectivism: the position that judgments of facts and/or judgments of values are typically grounded on a set of background assumptions that render those judgments non-absolute and conditional on the background

Philology: the humanistic study of languages and literature, usually ancient or classical, that focuses on word-origins, linguistic styles, and criticism

Problem of Evil: the philosophical question of why evil exists, as formulated typically within a monotheistic framework

Resentment: an especially poisonous sentiment, in Nietzsche's opinion, found typically in those who lack power or who lack spiritual strength

"Revaluation of all values": Nietzsche's call for the reconsideration of any given society's prevailing value-system, with the goal of instituting increasingly more healthy values

Slave Morality: a general style of moral thinking that derives its values by reacting to a perceived threat by (stronger) others in a defensive manner, such as to define its values as "other" than those of the threatening forces or peoples

Superhuman: *see Übermensch*

Theodicy: a theological mode of explanation that operates on the assumption that God exists, wherein God's moral reasons for allowing evil to exist are postulated

Thing-in-itself: the being of whatever exists as it is "in itself," as it stands independently of all finite perspectives

Übermensch: the "superhuman" type of being which, in Nietzsche's view, is super-healthy and expresses a fundamentally victorious attitude, and which consequently lives closely in touch with the nature of life and existence

Will-to-Power: a principle that Nietzsche uses to explain, depending upon the context, the nature of human behavior, the nature of life energies, or the nature of existence itself; the will-to-power is a drive for ever-increasing expansion and strength of one kind or another

Zarathustra: historically, the ancient prophet of Zoroastrianism – a religion that originated in Iran; also, the main character in Nietzsche's *Thus Spoke Zarathustra*. Nietzsche's Zarathustra partially exemplifies and partially heralds the ideally healthy condition that Nietzsche prescribes for future cultures.

Notes

1 One of these will be described in Chapter 3.

2 Some Nietzsche scholars draw our attention to the influence of Roman satire on key sections of his famous book, *Thus Spoke Zarathustra*. For example, see Kathleen M. Higgins, *Nietzsche's Zarathustra* (Philadelphia: Temple University Press, 1987), Chapter 7, where she discusses the influence of Lucius Apuleius (*c*.123–*c*.170), author of *The Golden Ass* (or *Transformations* [*Metamorphoseos*]).

3 In 1854, Wagner sent Schopenhauer a copy of his *Der Ring des Nibelungen* "with admiration and gratitude." Nietzsche was still a youngster at the time.

4 Nietzsche also felt that Wagner had insulted him, rather embarrassingly, by offering to others unjustified speculations about the sexual causes of his poor health. See Siegfried Mandel's *Nietzsche and the Jews* (New York: Prometheus Books, 1998), "The Deadly Insult," p. 118. See also Joachim Köhler's *Nietzsche and Wagner – A Lesson in Subjugation* (New Haven, CN and London: Yale University Press, 1998), "A Mortal Insult," pp. 147ff.

5 The excerpt is from Donne's *Meditation 17*.

6 In the twentieth century alone, the mind-numbing number of people deliberately killed for an assortment of ideological and religious reasons – an estimated 80 million – is nothing less than staggering. For a discussion of this, see Zbigniew Brzezinski, *Out of Control – Global Turmoil on the Eve of the 21st Century* (New York: Collier Books, Macmillan Publishing Company, 1993), especially "Part I – The Politics of Organized Insanity."

7   The phrase, "through a glass darkly," is from St. Paul (1 Corinthians 13: 12), where it is suggested that during our earthly lives, we humans can perceive and understand the universe and ourselves only very imperfectly, although in the next life we will behold the truth, when we see ourselves as God sees us. Kant's philosophy preserves a similar faith.

8   Arthur Schopenhauer, *The World as Will and Representation*, Vol. I, §28.

9   In *Beyond Good and Evil*, §17, Nietzsche foreshadows an aspect of Freud's conception of the "id." The word "id" means "it" in Latin, and it signifies for Freud a part of one's mental life – the seat of one's instinctual desires – that remains alien and mostly impervious to conscious introspection. The id is an amoral, instinctual part of ourselves that we cannot easily admit as being a real part of ourselves. Hence within us, it remains as an "it," or as an "other," to our conscious, generally law-abiding, selves.

10 Johann Gottlieb Fichte, *The Vocation of Man*, Book III, "Faith," Part II.

11 The mythical image of the worm or snake biting its own tail – the Ouroboros – aptly symbolizes the Nietzschean understanding of the universe. In Nietzsche's vision, we encounter nothing more than a field of energy that is self-contained and endlessly recycling.

12 Schopenhauer offers a paradigm image:

> The most glaring example of this kind is provided by the bulldog-ant of Australia: when one cuts it in half, a fight begins between the head and the tail – each attacks the other with bites and stings, and this struggle goes on bravely for half an hour, until they die, or are carried away by other ants. This happens every time. (*The World as Will and Representation*, Vol. I, §27)

13 Schopenhauer, *The World as Will and Representation*, Vol. I, §63. Schopenhauer advances this judgment under the assumption of traditional Christian moral values. If one were to abandon these values, as Nietzsche does, then the conclusion that human beings have a low worth would not obviously follow.

14 Ibid. The word "his" in the above excerpt is intended generally to mean "his or her."

15 This can refer to Schopenhauer's standpoint of moral awareness, where we adopt the perspective of humanity in general and become immersed in the sins and suffering of the world as a whole.

16 This can refer to Schopenhauer's standpoint of ascetic awareness and the "denial of the will," where we renounce the daily lifestyle of typical human culture. Since many of the ascetics that Schopenhauer discusses believed in God (as does the saint), the thought that the saint here represents "ascetic consciousness" is consistent with Schopenhauer's texts.

17 Nietzsche, *Thus Spoke Zarathustra*, "Zarathustra's Prologue," §2.

18 There is debate about whether Nietzsche concerned himself with the plight of humanity, in general, or only with a select group of extremely healthy people. When Zarathustra starts his spiritual journey, he says that "he loves people," but by the end of *Thus Spoke Zarathustra*, he gravitates to a small subset of "higher" ones – people who represent the best that the existing culture can offer. There is some literary evidence that Nietzsche nonetheless had general human interests in mind here, because one of the probable inspirations for the end of the book, Goethe's poem "*Die Geheimnisse*" ("The Secrets"), describes a Zarathustra-like leader named "Humanus" (representing the essence of humanity) who addresses a set of twelve representatives of the world's nations or religions.

For a synopsis of this poem, along with suggestions of its connection to the symbolism of Martin Luther's "rose and cross" coat of arms, see Karl Löwith's *From Hegel to Nietzsche* [1941] (Garden City, New York: Anchor Books, 1967), Introduction, §2, "Rose and Cross." For Luther's own explanation of his "rose and cross" symbolism, see his letter sent from Coburg Castle to Lazarus Spengler, 8 July, 1530. Nietzsche's Zarathustra finally crowns himself with a wreath of roses – one that replaces the wreath of ivy that he wore as a mere scholar.

19 Nietzsche's saint, as described in *Zarathustra*, has noticeably detached himself from the ordinary social world of the market place. St. Francis of Assisi can be seen as a related inspirational figure for

Nietzsche's Zarathustra, for there are striking parallels between Zarathustra's (and Nietzsche's) experiences and those of St. Francis. To begin, the latter was of weak physical constitution, but remained very strong-willed. Moreover, St. Francis was once labelled a heretic, he was accompanied by a falcon (Zarathustra was accompanied by an eagle), he called himself "God's fool" and "Brother Ass," he was disillusioned by the materialistic society that eventually infiltrated his following, he retired into caves for reclusive meditation, he often wept bitterly, he was descended upon by a flock of birds at a point of enlightenment (*Zarathustra* ends with this kind of event), he was reputed to have sung troubadour songs when young, he devoted his life to a feminized ideal which in Francis's case was "Lady Poverty," and he fought a spiritual battle against the desires of the flesh. One might go so far as to say that Nietzsche identified rather strongly with St. Francis's trials and redemption through suffering. If we ask the question, "Who is Nietzsche's Zarathustra?," much is revealed by regarding St. Francis as significantly informing Nietzsche's underlying model – despite St. Francis's Christian view that everyone is equal before God.

Nietzsche's Zarathustra is not a one-dimensional figure, however, and Zarathustra is more of an artistically-formed composite, like a compacted dream-image. Strong inspirational parallels also obtain between Zarathustra and possibly the greatest alchemist of all time, Paracelsus (Philippus Aureolus Theophrastus Bombast von Hohenheim, 1493–1541). Paracelsus, from Switzerland (Nietzsche referred to himself as "Swiss"), attacked the greediness of the apothecaries, rebelled against authority and established book learning, traveled with a group of devoted followers, was perceived to be a charlatan by many, and upheld noble values and piety. Paracelsus also developed, interestingly enough, a treatment for syphilis.

20 Ulrich von Wilamowitz-Möllendorf (1848–1931) – a young scholar who would later become a great German philologist – immediately attacked Nietzsche's book in a thirty-two-page pamphlet sarcastically titled *Philology of the Future*.

21 During his time as a professor of classics, Nietzsche taught courses in the Greek lyric poets, the Greek dramatists, Latin grammar, Hesiod,

the Pre-Socratic philosophers, Plato's *Dialogues*, and Greek and Roman rhetoric.

22 For example, see *Thus Spoke Zarathustra*, Part II, "On the Virtuous." Nietzsche's alienation from the values of the market place is reflected in his subtitle of the book, as one "for all and none." This is evident from Part IV, "On the Higher Person," §1, where Zarathustra states, "I stood in the market place; and as I spoke to all, I spoke to none."

23 Nietzsche, *The Birth of Tragedy*, §16.

24 As a paradigmatic image, we can recall the fierce and uncontrollable anger of Achilles, which was not considered to be excessive, but instead understandable and natural for his military situation.

25 This basic idea is also expressed in the "First Noble Truth" of Buddhism. Within the Buddhist context, it is observed that life contains aspects that tend to make it "sour" or frustrating, such as sickness, old age, and death.

26 Nietzsche, *The Birth of Tragedy*, §2.

27 This style of three-fold analysis was common in the late eighteenth and nineteenth centuries, and it was inspired by the three-fold form of the logical syllogism which Kant used to structure synoptically his theory of knowledge. For instance, Friedrich Schiller (who was inspired by Kant), divided human development into the sensory, aesthetic, and intellectual phases; Hegel (among tens of other such triads) divided the world of art into the "symbolic, classical, and romantic" periods; Marx famously divided economic history into feudal, capitalist, and communist periods. Nietzsche followed suit in his analysis of world history, using a pre-Greek, classical Greek, and post-Greek triad.

28 Nietzsche, *The Birth of Tragedy*, §18.

29 The German word "*Lust*" is usually translated as "joy" or "pleasure" in the sense of suggesting "merriment" and "festivity." Given, however, the ecstatic component of the experience Nietzsche describes when one becomes one with life-energies, this usual translation does not fully convey the power of the experience – one which, owing to its tapping into the strongest life-energy surges that humans experience, has distinctively orgasmic associations. The

pleasure at the heart of existence, in other words, is felt through a pleasure that resonates sexually.

30 Nietzsche, *The Birth of Tragedy*, §17. Nietzsche refers indiscriminately to both a thrill in "existence" and a thrill in "life," speaking of them here as if life and existence were one and the same. This identity between "existence-affirmation" and "life-affirmation" will be discussed critically in Chapter 6.

31 Ibid., §7.

32 Recall Schopenhauer's view (reiterated here by Nietzsche) that the principle of sufficient reason – a mode of dissective, integrative, and fundamentally literalistic interpretation that we ourselves project – is the cause of all individuation, and hence, a reason why we perceive a fragmented world of conflicting individuals.

33 Nietzsche, *The Birth of Tragedy*, §10.

34 The strategy of achieving greater wisdom by expanding one's finite perspective to cosmic levels has a long history in world philosophies. Among the views of this type that strongly influenced the early nineteenth-century philosophical world was that of the seventeenth-century Jewish philosopher, Benedict (Baruch) Spinoza (1632–77). See his *Ethics* (1677).

35 In his later thought, Nietzsche claimed that he no longer aspired to experience a "metaphysical comfort" through a transcendent, or extraordinary, mode of awareness, and maintained instead that "you ought to learn the art of *this-worldly* comfort first; you ought to learn to laugh" ("Attempt at Self-Criticism," Nietzsche's Preface to the 1886 reissue of *The Birth of Tragedy*).

36 An illuminating example is the "high-minded" or "great-souled" person (*megalopsychos*) who stands at the pinnacle of Aristotle's ethical vision. As a consequence of this type of person's rational and tempered quality, such a person, although willing to face great risks, is fundamentally "not fond of risks" (*Nichomachean Ethics*, 1124b). Nietzsche's superhuman ideal, in contrast, urges that one make danger "one's vocation" and love the idea of taking risks in a daredevil fashion.

37 Nietzsche, *The Birth of Tragedy*, §19.

38 Ibid., §18.

39   Ibid., §19.

40   Ibid., §17.

41   Ibid., §17.

42   This problem also has a practical correlate in Nietzsche's thought. As a leading voice of insubordination, he intends to be the master voice for all those who despise servitude to any masters or leaders.

43   Nietzsche, *The Birth of Tragedy*, §15.

44   Standing in thought-provoking contrast to this quote is a remark from *Thus Spoke Zarathustra*, "On Self-Overcoming," where Nietzsche claims that indirect, seductive approaches are weaker than the direct, head-on, and presumably more truthful approaches. One might reconcile the two remarks by saying that when one approaches the dangerous and overwhelming reality that is mother nature, one needs to be cautious, which is to say that here, the straightforward lance of reason – the traditional tool of "the scholar," as Nietzsche sees it – is not regarded as strong enough to pin down the truth.

45   For instance, Nietzsche suggests that in some central cases, if we examine the history of the situation, "humility" becomes a mask for "cowardice," and the "belief in justice" becomes a mask for "hope for revenge." See his *On the Genealogy of Morals*, First Essay, §14.

46   Nietzsche, *On the Genealogy of Morals*, First Essay, §17.

47   Nietzsche, "On Truth and Lie in a Morally-Disengaged Sense."

48   Under this interpretation, one need not ascribe an inconsistent "there is no truth" thesis to Nietzsche in this early essay, and hence overlook its importance as an expression of the generally Kantian outlook that Nietzsche had inherited from Schopenhauer. When Nietzsche asks, "What, then is truth?" he is best interpreted as asking about the "truths" we tend to take for granted in our everyday lives, rather than about the nature of truth itself.

49   Immanuel Kant, *Critique of Pure Reason* (A42/B59).

50   Nietzsche criticizes the tendencies that narrow down a person to the point of absurd specialization (see *Thus Spoke Zarathustra*, "On Redemption") and he refers to those who are, as he says, nothing but a large "eye" or a large "ear," as "inverse cripples." These people – among whom, Nietzsche acknowledges, some have been called "geniuses" – are not crippled people who lack an arm or a leg, or an

ear, but who are nothing more than an arm, or a leg, or an ear. One wonders, then, how Nietzsche would have assessed the impressionist paintings of his contemporary, Claude Monet (1840–1926), whom yet another contemporary, Paul Cézanne (1839–1906) said was "just an eye, but what an eye!"

51 Friedrich Schiller, *On the Aesthetic Education of Humanity*, Sixth Letter.

52 Karl Marx, *Manifesto of the Communist Party*, "Bourgeois and Proletariat."

53 Schiller, *On the Aesthetic Education of Humanity*, Sixth Letter. As noted above in the discussion of Nietzsche's *Birth of Tragedy*, this effort to return to the classical Greeks was influenced by the writings of Johann Winckelmann (1717–68), whose articles and books on classical Greek art (especially sculpture) portrayed Greek culture as one of humanity's healthiest and most beautiful manifestations.

54 Such questions arose in the philosophical area called "hermeneutics" or "theory of interpretation." Initially, the assumption was that one could learn ancient Greek, absorb as much as one could about Greek cultural history, actively put aside one's present-day influences, and reach a clear understanding of what the Greek cultural atmosphere was like. As reflections within the theory of interpretation continued, the view that one can never transcend one's own time period became increasingly influential. Some of the key figures in the history of hermeneutics implicitly referred to here are Friedrich Schleiermacher (1768–1834), Wilhelm Dilthey (1833–1911), and Martin Heidegger (1889–1976).

55 This tension arises in *The Birth of Tragedy*, where Nietzsche considers resurrecting the Dionysian-Greek spirit in a particularly "German" way – one that would include the music of Richard Wagner and the use of the German mythology.

56 In 1804, F. W. J. Schelling refers to this idea (in connection with the crucifixion) in his lectures on the philosophy of art; in 1807, G. W. F. Hegel uses the phrase "God is dead" several times in his *Phenomenology of Spirit*.

57 See the section on the "Unhappy Consciousness" in Hegel's *Phenomenology of Spirit*, especially §225. The "dark night of the soul"

imagery is from St. John of the Cross (1542–91). See the complete text of his *Ascent of Mt. Carmel* (1578–88).

58   Strong expressions of, and general interests in, nihilism often follow times of war. In the wake of the First World War, the Dada movement in Switzerland expressed a nihilistic protest against the technological style of reason that appeared to constitute the worldviews responsible for the European devastation; after the Second World War, intellectual interest in nihilism increased in both Germany and Japan.

59   In an autobiographical sketch written when he was a teenager (1858), Nietzsche described his reaction to his father's death:

> When I woke up that morning, I heard loud crying and sobbing all around me. My dear mother entered in tears and cried out, wailing, "Oh God! My dear Ludwig is dead!" Although I was still young and inexperienced, I did have some idea of death; I was seized by the thought of being forever separated from my beloved father, and I cried bitterly.
>
> The days following passed by in tears and in preparation for the burial. Oh God! I had become a fatherless orphan, and my mother had become a widow! – On 2 August the earthly remains of my dear father were entrusted into the womb of the earth… At one in the afternoon the ceremony began with a full tolling of the bells. Oh, the sound of those stifling bells will never leave my ears, and I will never forget the gloomy sounding melody of the hymn *Jesu meine Zuversicht* [Jesus, my Confidence]. ("From my Life" ["*Aus meinem Leben*"])

Nietzsche soon thereafter (at the end of January 1850) had a dream, which he described as follows:

> During that time I once dreamed that I heard the church organ playing, as if it were a funeral. When I went to see what was happening, a grave suddenly opened up, and my father emerged, dressed in burial clothes. He hurries into the church and returns quickly again with a small child in his arms. The grave-mound opens up, he climbs in and the cover sinks back

over the opening. The roaring sound of the organ goes silent and I wake up. – The next day little Joseph [Nietzsche's two-year-old brother] is suddenly unwell, goes into convulsions, and dies within a few hours. Our pain is terrible. My dream was completely realized. The little body was laid in the arms of my father. – With this double misfortune God in heaven was our single consolation and refuge. ("From my Life" ["*Aus meinem Leben*"])

60 See, for example, Nietzsche's discussion in *The Antichrist*, §39, where he claims that the motivating force at the root of Christianity is a "hatred of reality." This theme will be discussed further in Chapter 6, in the section on "existence-affirmation." We will see that the gap between "what is" and "what ought to be" tends to widen in proportion to one's dissatisfaction with "what is."

61 Nietzsche, *The Antichrist*, §18.

62 The main animal urges Nietzsche identifies are "sex," "the lust to rule," and "selfishness." See *Thus Spoke Zarathustra*, Part III, "The Three Evils."

63 Nietzsche expressed a similar idea in *The Birth of Tragedy*, except that the cause of the objectionable human condition was not said to be the Christian God, but Socratic, rationalistic thinking taken to the extreme. In both of his analyses, he identifies forces that suppress and constrict the "feral" or "wildlife" energies that he consistently refers to as "Dionysian."

64 Nietzsche, *On the Genealogy of Morals*, Second Essay, §22.

65 Nietzsche, *Thus Spoke Zarathustra*, Fourth Part, "The Ugliest Man." In *Ecce Homo*, Nietzsche said of himself that "I am by far the most awful human being that has so far existed; this does not preclude the possibility that I shall be the most beneficial" (*Ecce Homo*, "Why I am an Inevitability," §2). Nietzsche said this, presumably, because he believed that the truths he had to convey were "awful." One would suspect that these were the truths that "God is dead" (i.e., Nietzsche himself is one important "murderer" of God), the doctrine of the "will to power," the doctrine of the "superhuman," and the "doctrine of eternal recurrence."

66 One of the archetypal characters in *Thus Spoke Zarathustra* is a tightrope walker, who is referred to as "lamefoot." That the name "Oedipus" means "swollen foot" and the fact that this classical character famously killed his father and married his mother supports the idea that understanding Nietzsche requires us to investigate psychologically the "death-of-the-father" theme, given the centrality of the "death of God" theme in Nietzsche's work. For Nietzsche, the tightrope walker is celebrated as one who lives dangerously, but who inevitably goes down as well.

Nietzsche clearly idealizes and inflates both father and mother figures within his thought. He emphasizes on the one hand that the absolute father figure (God) must be killed, and on the other that one should seek reunification and absorption into the absolute mother figure (viz., the "eternal-feminine" or "mother nature" or Moira, the impersonal Greek goddess of fate [cf. *amor fati* in Nietzsche], whose Roman correlate is Parca, which means "birth"). The "death of God" theme and the "Nietzsche and woman" theme are thus two sides of the same coin.

67 The connection made here is an extended one. For the more psychoanalytically focused details of Freud's view, see his *Introductory Lectures on Psychoanalysis*, Chapter XXI, "The Development of the Libido." Freud mentions here that if a person does not reconcile the tensions of the Oedipus Complex, then the (male) person can become neurotic, and can remain bowed beneath his father's authority throughout his life. On his view, the rules of society eventually take the place of the father's authority and dominate as a "superego" within a person's psyche. The striving for self-definition as an individual thus transforms into a conflict between individuality (me) and sociality (in Heidegger's terms "the They" [*das Man*]) – a conflict which is a keynote of Nietzsche's philosophy.

68 An accurate description of this kind of perspectival impasse can be found in R. D. Laing's *Knots* (New York: Vintage Books, 1970), pp. 5–6.

69 The reference is to the prayers recited or sung at a Christian mass for the dead. More typically, the words are "*requiem aeternam dona ei (eis), Domine*" (eternal rest grant unto him/her (them), O Lord).

70 Nietzsche, *The Gay Science*, §125.

71 Nietzsche, *Thus Spoke Zarathustra*, Zarathustra's Prologue, §5.

72 Nietzsche, *Ecce Homo*, "Why I Write Such Good Books," §1.

73 Ibid., "Why I am an Inevitability," §1. In his notebooks of the same year (1888) [§107], Nietzsche referred to Wagner as an "inevitability" (*ein Schicksal*; or "destiny") as well, except that it was in the more limited context of his reflections on Wagner's subsequent influence on German culture.

74 Ibid., §2.

75 Nietzsche, *The Gay Science*, Book Three, §108.

76 Nietzsche, *Human, All-Too-Human*, Part II, "The Wanderer and his Shadow," §14.

77 Nietzsche, *The Gay Science*, Book Three, §109.

78 Nietzsche, *Twilight of the Idols*, "Skirmishes of an Untimely Man," §7. The emphasis on the word "chance" is in the original.

79 Nietzsche, *Daybreak: Thoughts on the Prejudices of Morality*, Book II, §130.

80 Nietzsche's particular version of this "life-focused" outlook is complicated by the influential development of physiology in Germany after 1830, and his discussions of "life" often tend towards physiological formulations. Nietzsche's association of "life" with the conditions especially germane to development, growth, breaking through one's former limits, and metamorphosis – as opposed to the conditions for biological balance and homeostasis – reveal within his thought, nonetheless, the predominance of the teleological, or progress-oriented, mentality that prevailed during the nineteenth century in general.

81 Nietzsche, *The Birth of Tragedy*, "Attempt at a Self-Criticism," §5.

82 Just as Immanuel Kant believed that logical thinking, along with spatial and temporal ordering, was an inescapable aspect of our human style of interpreting the world, Nietzsche believed that "immoral" behavior is an inescapable aspect of our style of interpretation as living beings.

83 In his postulation of the Oedipus Complex, Sigmund Freud asserted much the same thing. The doctrine of original sin is also echoed here.

84 Nietzsche, *Beyond Good and Evil – Prelude to a Philosophy of the Future*, "What is Distinguished," §259.

85 Nietzsche, *On the Genealogy of Morals*, Second Essay, §11.

86 There were some pre-Nietzschean efforts to formulate perspectives that were "beyond" or "above" the traditional "moral" outlooks, insofar as these outlooks were considered negatively, as being either too rigidly mechanical, overly rule-governed, and/or morally uninspiring (i.e., as not expressing the "true" moral spirit). One example is in Hegel's early writings (e.g., "The Spirit of Christianity," 1797), where he stated that via the feeling of love, all thought of [Kantian] duties vanishes, and one rises above the whole [mechanically defined] sphere of justice and injustice. A slightly more extreme example is in the writings of Søren Kierkegaard (1813–55), who characterized the paradoxical and incomprehensible "religious" perspective as one located beyond the rationally-grounded and rule-governed "ethical" perspective. He referred to this as the "teleological suspension of the ethical" in *Fear and Trembling* (1843).

87 Nietzsche, *Twilight of the Idols*, "Morality as Anti-Nature," §5.

88 Nietzsche, *Thus Spoke Zarathustra*, Part II, "On Self-Overcoming."

89 In *The Birth of Tragedy*, §21, Nietzsche also invokes this image of a person who is located at the "heart of life":

> If a person put his ear, so to speak, upon the heart chamber of the world-will, and felt the furious craving for existence, pouring out from there into all of the veins of the world, as a thundering river or as the softest sprinkle of stream, how could he not suddenly break into pieces?

This excerpt, and the one cited above from *Thus Spoke Zarathustra*, shows that one of the key thoughts in Nietzsche's philosophy – the idea of life-affirmation – is linked with the experience of feeling the surging and potentially self-disintegrating energies of life within oneself. It reveals also that Nietzsche's early studies of the experience of dramatic tragedy (where he discovers this experience of life) are central to understanding his philosophy.

90 Nietzsche, *Beyond Good and Evil*, §13.

91 Nietzsche, *The Antichrist*, §6.

92 Nietzsche, *Twilight of the Idols*, "The Problem of Socrates," §9.

93 Nietzsche, Notebook excerpt from 1885, §1067. The excerpt is memorable, but it should be kept in mind that it remains a notebook entry, and that its main value here is to convey the chilling atmosphere of Nietzsche's atheistic vision, which he expressed in various ways.

94 Nietzsche, "On Truth and Lie in a Morally-Disengaged Sense."

95 A cluster of words characterizes the atmosphere of the perspective at hand. The standpoint is "dislocated," "disconnected," "dissociated," "disengaged," and "detached." One of the prominent feelings that Nietzsche's philosophy conveys is one of dislocation. It is Nietzsche as the wanderer, the gypsy, the homeless, the alienated, and "the one who is different."

96 Here, life is said to be "immoral," rather than "amoral." Both characterizations fit, but Nietzsche tends to use the former term. As a literary gauge for appreciating the general difference between an "immoral" and an "amoral" consciousness – as they represent nineteenth vs. twentieth-century problematics, respectively – we can contrast Dostoevski's Raskolnikov (who critically ponders the significance of moral contexts) with Camus's Merseult (who simply seems to lack sensitivity to moral contexts). David Hudson pointed out to me in conversation this useful contrast between *Crime and Punishment* (1866) and *The Stranger* (1946).

97 Nietzsche, *Ecce Homo*, "Why I am so Wise," §2.

98 Ibid., "Thus Spoke Zarathustra," §1.

99 Nietzsche, *The Gay Science*, Book Four, §341.

100 Kathleen Higgins develops the philosophical connection between Descartes and Nietzsche within this context. See her *Comic Relief – Nietzsche's Gay Science* (Oxford: Oxford University Press, 2000), Chapter Six.

101 Nietzsche, *On the Genealogy of Morals*, Third Essay, §14.

102 The German word *Übermensch* translates literally as "over-person" or "over-human," but this translation does not convey the meaning well. Some translate it into English as "overman," since "over" suggests both the idea of "looking down" or "being above" in semantic fusion with the idea of "crossing over." The German word

"*Mensch*," though, refers to people in general, and not to men in particular, so "overman" has a sexist overtone. (This overtone might not have been particularly objectionable to Nietzsche.) The term "*Übermensch*" also suggests the perspective of someone who is located in the balcony of life's theater, looking down upon the stage; or it suggests someone who is in the play itself, watching himself or herself in the performance imaginatively from above. In each case there is a perspectival "distance" from the ordinary scene. The present translation of "*Übermensch*" as "superhuman" suggests that this being possesses extraordinary willpower – so much so as to be qualitatively different in consciousness, in contrast to most people.

103 Nietzsche, *Beyond Good and Evil*, §56.

104 This is a quote from Mother Theresa, mentioned in the final homily of Cardinal O'Connor of New York, given at St. Patrick's Cathedral, 20 February 2000. A related attitude is expressed by St. Paul: "whatever does not proceed from faith, is sin" (Romans 14:23).

105 Nietzsche, *Ecce Homo*, "Why I am an Inevitability," §9.

106 Nietzsche, Notebook excerpt from March–June 1888, §1052. This excerpt from 1888 mirrors Nietzsche's account of the aesthetic experience of tragedy described sixteen years earlier in *The Birth of Tragedy*, §7 (quoted earlier), and is evidence of a strong continuity in his thought with respect to his interpretation of the Greeks.

107 Nietzsche, *Ecce Homo*, "Why I Write Such Good Books," §1.

108 In *Ecce Homo*, Nietzsche mentioned that "one could consider the whole of *Zarathustra* as music" (*Ecce Homo*, "Thus Spoke Zarathustra," §1). If we recall Nietzsche's earlier interest in helping to inspire a more life-affirming "tragic culture," and his celebration of Bach, Beethoven, and Wagner in *The Birth of Tragedy* as artistic forces supportive of this end, then *Zarathustra* "as music" can be read as a continuation of this project of cultural revision. The famous doctrines of the superhuman, the eternal recurrence, the will-to-power, and the death of God, consequently would express a fundamentally tragic sense of life, as it stands tempered and amalgamated with a stronger, down-to-earth sense of life-affirmation, and its accompanying laughter, dancing, and joyous thrill – which is to say that Nietzschean laughter is informed by life's difficulties.

109 Nietzsche, *Human, All-Too-Human*, "Assorted Opinions and Maxims," §180. Nietzsche is inspired here by Wagner's concept of the "total-artwork" (*Gesamtkunstwerk*), which advocated an amalgamation of all operatic devices – music, verse, staging – into a complete whole. See Wagner's *Opera and Drama* (*Oper und Drama* [1850–51]) and *The Artwork of the Future* (*Das Kunstwerk der Zukunft* [1849]), whose title, incidentally, supplies material for Nietzsche's later preoccupation with future philosophy and future ideals.

110 See, for example, *Thus Spoke Zarathustra*, Part II, "On Priests."

111 As the opposite of the superhuman type, Nietzsche described at the very beginning of *Thus Spoke Zarathustra*, the "last man" (*der letzte Mensch*) – a type of temperate person who does not push anything to excess, and who aims at a pleasurably balanced life. Such a person might enjoy a pleasant walk in the hills, but would never dare to go mountain-climbing, lest a fatal accident occur. Such a person would live carefully, and not very dangerously, in other words. If one interprets Nietzsche's superhuman as a Dionysian antagonist to this moderate, temperate, proportionate, and balanced type of person (cf. Aristotle's doctrine of the mean), then one can import the ethics of hard work into the superhuman framework, and further link Nietzsche's superhuman with Kant's suggestion that we have a moral obligation to develop our talents significantly (see Kant's *Foundations of the Metaphysics of Morals*, Second Section) and, implicitly, commit ourselves to developing them extremely, and not only halfway, or merely "in moderation."

   At a greater extreme, Nietzsche's "last man" can be linked with idleness or laziness – the kinds of sin that brought down the cities of Sodom and Gomorrah, insofar as idleness and laziness generate a weakness of character that opens a person to temptation.

112 Nietzsche, *Ecce Homo*, "Why I Am So Wise," §2.

113 Nietzsche's *Thus Spoke Zarathustra – A Book for All and None*, when regarded as a work of confessional literature, illuminates the idea of "Nietzschean laughter" in the present context. One can imagine the reaction of a person, who, after having earnestly set forth a confession in a confessional booth, noticed afterwards that there had been no one in the priest's seat. The consequent laughter might be very

strong. The idea that "all the world's a stage" in the absence of an audience would be analogous.

114 Nietzsche, *The Gay Science*, §339.

115 Nietzsche, *Daybreak*, §170.

116 Nietzsche, *The Birth of Tragedy*, §3.

117 The Medusa, more thoroughly considered, is a complicated Janus-like image combining both Apollonian and Dionysian aspects, since Medusa was once a beautiful woman. In *The Birth of Tragedy*, Nietzsche emphasizes her Dionysian aspect.

118 The Medusa image is more important in Nietzsche's writings than an English-language reader might initially realize, though, since Walter Kaufmann's widely-used translation [1967] (along with Francis Golffing's earlier one [1956]) of *The Birth of Tragedy* renders the specific "*das Medusenhaupt*" more generically, as "Gorgon's head" (e.g., see §2).

119 Nietzsche, *The Gay Science*, Preface to Second Edition (1886).

120 Nietzsche, *The Birth of Tragedy*, §15.

121 The presence of mixed emotions, or ambivalence, or what sometimes appears to be contradictory perspectives on Nietzsche's part, can be understood in light of his fundamental insight that the quality of lived human experience typically involves complicated amalgams of feelings and judgments. This indicates that within concrete human awareness, metaphorical styles of thinking – those which can fuse manifestly opposite outlooks, as in the semantically-condensed images of dreams – are considered to be foundational. It also indicates that wisdom, considered as a style of discrimination among a set of interconnected variables, is regarded as a more existentially central thought-process than the atomized and abstracted styles of knowledge, all of which require that each element is definitionally self-contained.

122 Nietzsche, *Thus Spoke Zarathustra*, Fourth Part, "The Ugliest Man."

123 Nietzsche, *Beyond Good and Evil*, §40.

124 Nietzsche, Notebooks of March–June 1888 (§293).

125 Nietzsche, Notebooks of 1884 (§602). This excerpt illuminates Nietzsche's "profound superficiality" prescription of 1886 (see the Preface to *The Gay Science*).

126 Nietzsche often uses the intellectual strategy of dissolving a standardly accepted conceptual distinction in order to advance an alternative standpoint. In *The Gay Science* §103, for example, he claimed that if one recognizes that there are no "purposes" in the fabric of things, then one would realize that there are no "accidents" either.

127 Maudemarie Clark, in her *Nietzsche On Truth and Philosophy* (Cambridge: Cambridge University Press, 1990), offers a first-rate scholarly account of Nietzsche's development within this context. The distinction presented below between "perspectivism" and "interpretationism" is also indebted to the basic insights of Clark's study.

128 The reference here is to Kant, who asserted the identity of the transcendental object and transcendental subject in his *Critique of Pure Reason* (A109).

129 Nietzsche, Notebook entry, Spring–Fall, 1887 [§552].

130 Ibid.

131 Ibid. [§569].

132 In 1887, we encounter residual expressions of his earlier and prevailing view, such as *On the Genealogy of Morals*, Third Essay, §12, which carries a distinctively Kantian flavor. In contrast, we can note in the same year a notebook entry [§507] where Nietzsche states that the seemingly neutral distinction between the real and apparent world arises only on account of value postulations. A more radical statement – one expressive of the more purely "interpretationist" view – can be found in Nietzsche's notebooks of 1888 [§567]:

> The *perspective* therefore provides the character of the "appearance"! As if a world would still be left over after one subtracted the perspective! By doing that one would subtract *relativity*!

133 Charles F. Wallraff, translator of Karl Jaspers' *Nietzsche* (1935), and student of Jaspers in Heidelberg in 1935, used the term "interpretationism" to characterize his own views, as expressed in *Philosophical Theory and Psychological Fact* (Tucson: University of Arizona Press, 1961).

134 For a detailed scholarly analysis of the various competing formulations of Nietzsche's perspectivism, see Clark, Chapter 5, "Perspectivism."

135 Nietzsche, *Twilight of the Idols*, "'Reason' in Philosophy," §2. The idea that "reason" is a mode of falsification recalls Schopenhauer's

interpretation of the principle of sufficient reason. Here, the sensory flux takes the place of Schopenhauer's "thing-in-itself," both of which are believed to be falsified by means of reason.

136 Ibid., "How the 'True World' Finally Became a Fable."

137 This Nietzschean position was developed by Jean-Paul Sartre in his *Being and Nothingness* (1943). See the first section of his Introduction to that work, "I. The Phenomenon."

138 Among twentieth-century theories of linguistic meaning, and related to this Nietzschean position, Ludwig Wittgenstein (1889–1951) held that the meanings of words such as "pain" are not grounded upon references to each of our private, hidden-from-everyone-else (i.e., like inaccessible "thing-in-themselves") experiences. See Wittgenstein's much-discussed "beetle in the box" example in his *Philosophical Investigations* (1953), §293.

139 Nietzsche, *Twilight of the Idols*, "Maxims and Arrows," §27.

140 This image of the painted rice-cake is from Dogen, the thirteenth-century Japanese Zen master. The interpretation offered here of Nietzsche's views on "truth as an empty mask" in conjunction with his emphasis on "existence-affirmation" (as opposed to "life-affirmation") is inspired by Dogen.

141 See *The Tibetan Book for the Dead*, "The Twelfth Day."

142 Nietzsche, *Thus Spoke Zarathustra*, Part II, "On the Riffraff." A more abstract and far-reaching interpretation of this remark is that no human being can escape "the rabble," insofar as everyone's awareness is necessarily formed within some given cultural tradition and set of social and linguistic values. Nietzsche would not, then, simply be lamenting the presence of "the riffraff" or "the rabble" outside of himself in everyday society; he would be lamenting the presence of the currently imperfectly existing society within himself, as it constitutes his consciousness through the language he has learned and the cultural values he has necessarily absorbed as a matter of upbringing.

143 Ibid., Part III, "The Convalescent," §2.

144 At the end of *Thus Spoke Zarathustra*, we learn that feeling "pity" for even the most spiritually advanced types of people (which might include Nietzsche himself, and so we would also be speaking here of

self-pity) – along with pity for suffering in general – is the "final sin" that Zarathustra supposedly overcomes. One might ask why "pity" is accorded such a central place in Zarathustra's spiritual development, since there are many virtues and vices which color human experience.

Aristotle's theory of tragedy is of some significance here. For him, pity and fear in proportionate combination within the tragic experience operate homeopathically to clear the mind of those disturbing emotions themselves. He adds that pity is aroused by unmerited misfortune. Hence, if one regards the world as morally godless, as a stage, and as a tragedy, then one will experience pity in accord with this theory, and the therapeutic task will then be to use one's judgment in an effort to adopt a perspective through which the experience of potentially overwhelming pity can be controlled, and such that the experience of pity can be positively cathartic, rather than vicious and nihilistically debilitating. Whether Nietzsche completely overcame his feelings of self-pity is an open question.

145 Philip J. Ivanhoe suggested to me the phrase "affirmation of flourishing" as a synonym for "affirmation of health."

146 Nietzsche, *Ecce Homo*, "Why I am so Clever," §10.

147 Ibid., §9.

148 Ibid., "Thus Spoke Zarathustra," §6.

149 Given its attention to minute detail, Nietzsche's first expression of the doctrine of Eternal Recurrence (*The Gay Science,* §341), quoted earlier, was perhaps his strongest formulation.

150 Nietzsche, *Thus Spoke Zarathustra*, Part III, "The Seven Seals." It is worth noting that there is a reference to "seven seals" in Revelation 5:1. In that passage, the biblical image is of God who sits on a throne with a scroll that has been sealed with seven seals, upon which the future has been written.

151 See Walter Kaufmann, *The Portable Nietzsche* (New York: The Viking Press, 1968), p. 263.

152 Reprinted by permission of the publishers from *The Art of Shakespeare's Sonnets* by Helen Vendler (Cambridge, Mass.: The Belknap Press of Harvard University Press, Copyright © 1997 by the President and Fellows of Harvard College).

153 Albert Camus developed an outline for such a lifestyle in his conception of "the absurd lifestyle" in *The Myth of Sisyphus*. Camus's outlook resonates with the Japanese heroic tradition or "way of the warrior" (*bushido*), to the extent that this tradition also acknowledges the nobility of fighting a losing battle. In addition, Kierkegaard's "knight of faith" (see his *Fear and Trembling*) is also closely related to this idea.

154 Within the present Nietzschean, fundamentally atheistic, context, it should not escape our notice that the thought that "existence is a perfection," or that "it is better to be than not to be," is foundational to the ontological argument for God's existence. One might say that in some of his reflections, Nietzsche turns raw existence itself into God, or more precisely, into that which is absolutely "holy." See the excerpt from Nietzsche's notebooks, March–June 1888 [§1052] cited above.

155 Nietzsche, *The Antichrist*, §57.

156 This Nietzschean idea of reinterpreting everyday moments into works of art – the project of transforming them into "perfect moments" – was expressed in literary form by Jean-Paul Sartre in his novel, *Nausea* (1938).

157 In *Ecce Homo*, "Why I am so Clever," §1, Nietzsche states that he "never devoted any attention or time" to concepts such as "redemption" and "God." What he intends to say, since he speaks famously and repeatedly about the concept of "God," for instance, is that these concepts have been "spoiled" by Christianity, and have been perverted in their proper meaning. He made this point explicitly in *The Gay Science*, §335. For a classic statement of Nietzsche's own, alternative, conception of redemption, see *Thus Spoke Zarathustra*, Book II, "On Redemption."

As early as *Schopenhauer as Educator* (1874), §6, Nietzsche was fundamentally interested in redemption, going so far as to say that "humanity ought to seek out and create the favorable conditions" under which more redemptive people can be brought into existence. If one considers the root meaning of the German word "*Erlösung*" – the word which is translated into English as "redemption" – the clusters of meanings include "to release," "to loosen up," "to cast off," and "to remove." All of these suggest that the quest for redemption is a quest for a kind of freedom, and that Nietzsche is fundamentally interested in attaining a release from various kinds of bondage.

158 In *Ecce Homo*, "Daybreak," §1, he claimed that his "campaign against morality" began at the end of the decade, in his appropriately titled book, *Daybreak* (1880).

159 The term "theodicy" was introduced into philosophical currency by Leibniz, who was referred to above as maintaining that the world we live in is "the best of all possible worlds." Voltaire (1694–1778) memorably satirized this idea in *Candide* (1759).

160 Nietzsche, *The Case of Wagner*, §3.

161 Nietzsche's implicit reference here is to Jesus' story of the prodigal son (here, "the one who had been lost"). See Luke 15:11–32. The suggestion is that one "comes home" to the world as a whole by means of the attitude of life-affirmation described here.

162 Nietzsche, *Thus Spoke Zarathustra*, Part I, "On the Three Transformations."

163 Nietzsche, *Ecce Homo*, "Thus Spoke Zarathustra," §8.

164 Nietzsche, *The Genealogy of Morals*, Second Essay, §24.

165 Nietzsche at one point refers to a "thousand-year Zarathustra-Reich" (*Thus Spoke Zarathustra*, Part IV, "The Honey Offering"), which conveys associations between Zarathustra, Jesus, and Charlemagne. In terms of future projections, Revelation 20:1–10 refers to the "first resurrection" where it is said that Jesus, at some point in the future, will reign for one thousand years. In terms of past history, Charlemagne was crowned by Pope Leo III on Christmas Day, 800, to initiate the Holy Roman Empire that would last for 1000 years.

166 See Matthew 5:19–22.

167 Nietzsche, *Thus Spoke Zarathustra*, Part III, "On Old and New Tablets," §10.

168 This interpretation of Eternal Recurrence as the "recurrence of the different," rather than the "recurrence of the same" is offered by Gilles Deleuze in his book, *Nietzsche and Philosophy* (1962). The original thought is from Georg Simmel (*Schopenhauer and Nietzsche* [1907]), who, as a critique of Nietzsche's doctrine of the "recurrence of the

same," developed a mathematical example that embodied the continual occurrence of unique patterns.

169 Nietzsche, *The Antichrist*, §33.

170 *The Gay Science*, §290, has an especially detailed account of how one
can "give style" to one's character. The aesthetic justification of
suffering involves regarding suffering in the correct perspective; to
do this, one makes oneself into a sublime character.

171 Nietzsche, *Ecce Homo*, "Why I am an Inevitability," §1.

172 Independently of his sister's activities during the 1890s and the first
decade of the twentieth century, Nietzsche's writings were appreciated by a variety of groups that ranged across the political spectrum.
See Steven Aschheim's *The Nietzsche Legacy in Germany, 1890–1990*
(Berkeley and Los Angeles: University of California Press, 1992).

173 Nietzsche, *The Case of Wagner*, §5.

174 Nietzsche, *Ecce Homo*, "Why I am so Clever," §1.

175 Ibid., §5.

176 Ibid., "The Case of Wagner," §3.

177 Förster was known during Nietzsche's lifetime as someone who,
joined by Nietzsche's sister, attempted to establish an Aryan colony
in the remote, and "non-racially polluted," jungles of Paraguay – a
colony which they called "*Nueva Germania*" (New Germany) – and
with which Nietzsche wanted no connection whatsoever. For the
details of this colony's development and demise, see Ben
MacIntyre's *Forgotten Fatherland – In Search of Elisabeth Nietzsche*
(New York: Harper/Perennial, 1993). Wagner's anti-Semitism is
attested by his own writings.

178 Chamberlain, Wagner, and Hitler were all influenced by Joseph
Arthur Gobineau's mid-nineteenth-century book, *The Inequality of
Human Races* (1853–55) – a work which argued that the "Aryan"
peoples were racially superior to all others. Gobineau claimed that it
was essential to preserve a civilization's racial character, and that
intermixture between different groups should be minimized, lest
the vitality of the civilization be diluted and undermined. From
such typical claims issue the alleged connection between social
health and the maintenance of racial purity. Gobineau's book,
however, only reinforced Richard Wagner's already-existing anti-

Semitism. Wagner's essay, "Judaism in Music," was written in 1850 (and first published under a pseudonym) – at a time, it is worth adding, long before Nietzsche met him.

179 See Geoffrey George Field, *Houston Stewart Chamberlain: Prophet of Bayreuth* (Ph.D. Dissertation, Faculty of Political Science, Columbia University, 1972), pp. 102–104.

180 In January 1888, immediately after his collapse, he wrote a letter to Cosima Wagner which read, "Ariadne, I love you."

181 For example, Nietzsche's critical remarks often focus on a specific Jewish group (e.g., the Pharisees, whom he likens to "tarantulas"), rather than on the Jewish people as a whole.

182 See, for example, *Mein Kampf*, Vol. II, Chapter 17.

183 Hitler also used arguments that might have come directly from Nietzsche. For example, he referred to "the Jewish teachings of Marxism" which "reject the aristocratic principle of nature and put in place of the eternal prerogative of force and strength, the mass of numbers and their dead weight." *Mein Kampf*, Vol. I, Chapter 2. See, in comparison, Nietzsche's notebook entry from March–June 1888 (§53), which is almost identical in wording, although it is aimed at a different subject. I thank Geoffrey Roche for the discussion that directed me to this passage.

184 Nietzsche, *The Antichrist*, §38.

185 Hitler comparably used the word "parasite" [*Parasit*], to refer to the Jewish people (*Mein Kampf*, Vol. I, Chapter 11, "Nation and Race").

186 Nietzsche, *The Antichrist*, §42.

187 Ibid., §43.

188 Ibid., §46.

189 Nietzsche, *The Gay Science*, §40.

190 Nietzsche, *Thus Spoke Zarathustra*, Part III, "On the Virtue that Makes One Small," §3.

191 Nietzsche, *On the Genealogy of Morals*, Third Essay, §21.

192 Hitler stated that he was addressing a "spiritual pestilence, worse than the Black Death of times past" (*Mein Kampf*, Vol. I, Chapter 2, "Years of Study and Suffering in Vienna").

193 The idea of having to "wash oneself clean with contaminated water" reveals a more general philosophical condition. One might

ask, for instance, how it is possible to arrive at a universally-valid view if the language one inherits is filled with the limiting prejudgments and valuations of one's specific historical time period or specific culture. Similarly, one can ask how it is possible to express a non-sexist viewpoint if the language one inherits is itself permeated with sexism.

194 Nietzsche, *Thus Spoke Zarathustra*, Part II, "On Human Cleverness."

195 Ibid., "Zarathustra's Prologue," §3.

196 Nietzsche, *Beyond Good and Evil*, "What is Distinguished," §260.

197 Nietzsche, *On the Genealogy of Morals*, Third Essay, §16.

198 Nietzsche made this comparison between himself (as "Zarathustra") and the Jewish people. See *Thus Spoke Zarathustra*, Part IV, "The Shadow." It goes along with his many references to himself as a "wanderer."

199 Nietzsche, *Ecce Homo*, "Why I am so Clever," §3.

200 The title of Nietzsche's *The Gay Science* was inspired by the twelfth-century, southern Provence troubadours.

201 More generally speaking, there is also a more distant connection – via the idea of decapitation – to the Medusa image that appears in Nietzsche's writings.

202 On some accounts of the Medusa myth, moreover, Perseus turns Medusa into stone by leading her to behold her own reflection. Sartre's theory of consciousness is strangely parallel with this idea. According to him, to think explicitly about anything, requires that one hold it fast before one's consciousness and therefore objectify it (i.e., turn it into "stone"). So when one explicitly thinks about oneself (or about anything else), one must negate the living activity of oneself-as-thinker by turning oneself into an object of thought (i.e., turn oneself into "stone"). Sartre's theory of consciousness, in effect, turns us all into Medusas.

203 See the subsection of the first chapter of Camus's *The Myth of Sisyphus*, "Absurd Walls."

204 Nietzsche, *Human, All-Too-Human*, "On First and Last Things," §2.

205 Epictetus, the Roman Stoic philosopher, captured this sentiment well, for he urged us to remember that when we grow fond of

something, the nature of the thing we are fond of should always be kept in mind. If we fall in love with a perishable being, such as a person, we must be prepared for the day when the person will die. See Epictetus, *Handbook*, §3.

206 Nietzsche's projection of the coming of the "superhuman" can be understood as a residual artifact of his prevailing nineteenth-century context. In other parts of his philosophy, as we have seen, Nietzsche observes only the continual recycling of the world's contents, which he believes do not aim towards any special end.

207 Nietzsche, Lectures on the Pre-Platonic Philosophers, "§10, Heraclitus."

208 If, however, one subjects the very idea of "health" to a genealogical-historical analysis, noting that different societies have had different conceptions of health, then one can challenge the foundational idea of "health" within the Nietzschean position itself.

209 In *Thus Spoke Zarathustra*, Book One, "On the Thousand and One Goals," Nietzsche states that the meaning of "human" is "*der Schätzende*" (the appraiser; the esteemer; the valuer; the evaluator; the assessor; the appreciator).

210 Nietzsche, *Ecce Homo*, "Why I am an Inevitability," §4.

211 Ibid., §2.

212 Eris is the Greek goddess of discord.

213 Shiva is the Vedic god of destruction.

Bibliography

Nietzsche's writings

Kritische Gesamtausgabe Briefwechsel, ed. G. Colli and M. Montinari, 24 vols. in 4 parts. Berlin: Walter de Gruyter, 1975

The Antichrist, trans. Walter Kaufmann, in *The Portable Nietzsche*, ed. Walter Kaufmann. New York: Viking Press, 1968

Beyond Good and Evil, trans. Walter Kaufmann. New York: Random House, 1966

The Birth of Tragedy, trans. Walter Kaufmann, in *The Birth of Tragedy and The Case of Wagner*. New York: Random House, 1967

The Case of Wagner, trans. Walter Kaufmann, in *The Birth of Tragedy and The Case of Wagner*. New York: Random House, 1967

Daybreak: Thoughts on the Prejudices of Morality, trans. R. J. Hollingdale. Cambridge: Cambridge University Press, 1982

Ecce Homo: How One Becomes What One Is, trans. Walter Kaufmann, in *On the Genealogy of Morals and Ecce Homo*. New York: Random House, 1967

The Gay Science, with a Prelude of Rhymes and an Appendix of Songs, trans. Walter Kaufmann. New York: Random House, 1974

Human, All Too Human: A Book for Free Spirits, trans. R. J. Hollingdale. Cambridge: Cambridge University Press, 1986

Nietzsche Contra Wagner, trans. Walter Kaufmann, in *The Portable Nietzsche*. New York: Viking Press, 1968

On the Genealogy of Morals, trans. Walter Kaufmann and R. J. Hollingdale, in *On the Genealogy of Morals and Ecce Homo*. New York: Random House, 1967

Philosophy in the Tragic Age of the Greeks, trans. Marianne Cowan. Chicago: Henry Regnery Company, 1962

Philosophy and Truth: Selections from Nietzsche's Notebooks of the Early 1870s, trans. and ed. Daniel Breazeale. Atlantic Highlands, NJ: Humanities Press, 1979

Thus Spoke Zarathustra, trans. Walter Kaufmann, in *The Portable Nietzsche*. New York: Viking Press, 1968

Twilight of the Idols, trans. Walter Kaufmann, in *The Portable Nietzsche*. New York: Viking Press, 1968

Untimely Meditations, trans. R. J. Hollingdale. Cambridge: Cambridge University Press, 1983

The Will to Power, trans. Walter Kaufmann. New York: Random House, 1967

Books about Nietzsche

Aschheim, Steven E. *The Nietzsche Legacy in Germany, 1890–1990.* Berkeley and Los Angeles: University of California Press, 1992

Clark, Maudemarie. *Nietzsche on Truth and Philosophy.* Cambridge: Cambridge University Press, 1990

Danto, Arthur C. *Nietzsche as Philosopher: An Original Study.* New York: Columbia University Press, 1965

Gilman, Sander L., ed., and David J. Parent, trans. *Conversations with Nietzsche: A Life in the Words of his Contemporaries.* New York: Oxford University Press, 1987

Hayman, Ronald. *Nietzsche, a Critical Life.* New York: Oxford University Press, 1980

Heidegger, Martin. *Nietzsche, Vol. I: The Will to Power as Art*, trans. David F. Krell. New York: Harper & Row, 1979

Nietzsche, Vol. II: The Eternal Recurrence of the Same, trans. David F. Krell. San Francisco: Harper & Row, 1984

Nietzsche, Vol. III.: Will to Power as Knowledge and as Metaphysics, trans. Joan Stambaugh and Frank Capuzzi. San Francisco: Harper & Row, 1986

Nietzsche, Vol. IV: Nihilism, trans. David F. Krell. New York: Harper & Row, 1982

Higgins, Kathleen Marie. *Nietzsche's Zarathustra*. Philadelphia: Temple University Press, 1987

Comic Relief – Nietzsche's Gay Science. Oxford University Press, 2000

Hollingdale, R. J. *Nietzsche*. London and New York: Routledge and Kegan Paul, 1973

Hunt, Lester H. *Nietzsche and the Origin of Virtue*. London: Routledge, 1991

Jaspers, Karl. *Nietzsche: An Introduction to the Understanding of His Philosophical Activity*, trans. Charles F. Wallraff and Frederick J. Schmitz. South Bend, IN: Regnery/Gateway, Inc., 1979

Jung, Carl G. *Nietzsche's "Zarathustra,"* ed. James L. Jarred. Princeton: Princeton University Press, 1988

Kaufmann, Walter. *Nietzsche: Philosopher, Psychologist, Antichrist*. Princeton: Princeton University Press, 1950

Klossowski, Pierre. *Nietzsche and the Vicious Circle*. London: Athlone, 1993

Lambert, Laurence. *Nietzsche's Teaching: An Interpretation of Thus Spoke Zarathustra*. New Haven, CT: Yale University Press, 1987

MacIntyre, Ben. *Forgotten Fatherland: The Search for Elisabeth Nietzsche*. London: Macmillan, 1992

Magnus, Bernd. *Nietzsche's Existential Imperative*. Bloomington, IN: Indiana University Press, 1978

Magnus, Bernd, Stanley Stewart, and Jean-Pierre Mileur. *Nietzsche's Case: Philosophy as/and Literature*. New York and London: Routledge, 1993

Nehamas, Alexander. *Nietzsche: Life as Literature*. Cambridge, MA: Harvard University Press, 1985

Parkes, Graham. *Composing the Soul: Reaches of Nietzsche's Psychology*. Chicago and London: University of Chicago Press, 1994

Pletch, Carl. *Young Nietzsche: Becoming a Genius*. New York: Free Press, 1991

Poellner, Peter. *Nietzsche and Metaphysics*. New York and London: Oxford University Press, 1995

Richardson, John. *Nietzsche's System*. New York: Oxford University Press, 1996

Rosen, Stanley. *The Mask of Enlightenment: Nietzsche's Zarathustra*. Cambridge: Cambridge University Press, 1995

Salomé, Lou. *Nietzsche*, ed. and trans. Siegfried Mandel. Redding Ridge, CT: Black Swan Books, Ltd., 1988

Schacht, Richard. *Nietzsche*. London: Routledge and Kegan Paul, 1983

Schrift, Alan D. *Nietzsche and the Question of Interpretation: Between Hermeneutics and Deconstruction*. New York: Routledge, 1990

Shapiro, Gary. *Nietzschean Narratives*. Bloomington, IN: Indiana University Press, 1989

Simmel, Georg. *Schopenhauer and Nietzsche*, trans. Helmut Loiskandle, Deena Weinstein, and Michael Weinstein. Urbana and Chicago: University of Illinois Press, 1991

Stambaugh, Joan. *The Problem of Time in Nietzsche*, trans. John F. Humphrey. Philadelphia: Bucknell University Press, 1987

White, Alan. *Within Nietzsche's Labyrinth*. New York and London: Routledge, 1990

Wilcox, John T. *Truth and Value in Nietzsche*. Ann Arbor, MI: University of Michigan Press, 1974

Young, Julian. *Nietzsche's Philosophy of Art*. Cambridge: Cambridge University Press, 1992

Collected essays on Nietzsche

Allison, David B., ed. *The New Nietzsche: Contemporary Styles of Interpretation*. Cambridge, MA: The MIT Press, 1985

Bloom, Harold., ed. *Modern Critical Views: Friedrich Nietzsche*. New York, New Haven, Philadelphia: Chelsea House Publishers, 1987

Janaway, Christopher., ed. *Willing and Nothingness: Schopenhauer as Nietzsche's Educator*. Oxford and New York: Clarendon Press, 1998

Koelb, Clayton., ed. *Nietzsche as Postmodernist: Essays Pro and Contra*. Albany, NY: State University of New York Press, 1990

Magnus, Bernd, and Higgins, Kathleen M., eds. *The Cambridge Companion to Nietzsche*. Cambridge: Cambridge University Press, 1996

Parkes, Graham, ed. *Nietzsche and Asian Thought*. Chicago: University of Chicago Press, 1991

Schacht, Richard, ed. *Nietzsche, Genealogy, Morality: Essays on Nietzsche's Genealogy of Morals*. Berkeley: University of California Press, 1994

Sedgwick, Peter R., ed. *Nietzsche: A Critical Reader*. Oxford, UK, and Cambridge, MA: Blackwell, 1995

Solomon, Robert, ed. *Nietzsche: A Collection of Critical Essays*. Garden City, NY: Anchor Books, 1973

Solomon, Robert C., and Higgins, Kathleen M., eds. *Reading Nietzsche*. New York and Oxford: Oxford University Press, 1988

Yovel, Yirmiyahu, ed. *Nietzsche as Affirmative Thinker*. Dordrecht: Martinus Nihoff Publishers, 1986

Related works

Camus, Albert. *The Myth of Sisyphus and Other Essays* [1942], trans. Justin O'Brien. New York: Vintage Books, 1955

David-Néel, Alexandra. *The Secret Oral Teachings in Tibetan Buddhist Sects*. San Francisco: City Lights Books, 1967

Epictetus. *Handbook of Epictetus* [*Enchiridion*], trans. Nicholas White. Indianapolis: Hackett Publishing Company, Inc., 1983

Fichte, Johann Gottlieb. *The Vocation of Man* [1800], trans. Roderick M. Chisholm. Indianapolis: The Bobbs-Merrill Company, Inc., 1956

Freud, Sigmund. *Introductory Lectures on Psychoanalysis* [1915–17], translated and edited by James Strachey. New York and London: W. W. Norton & Company, 1966

Hegel, G. W. F. *Phenomenology of Spirit* [1806], trans. A. V. Miller. Oxford: Oxford University Press, 1977

Hitler, Adolf. *Mein Kampf* [1925–26], trans. Ralph Manheim. London: Pimlico, 1992

Kant, Immanuel. *Critique of Pure Reason* [1781/87], trans. Norman Kemp Smith. New York: St. Martin's Press, 1965

Kant, Immanuel. *Foundations of the Metaphysics of Morals* [1785], trans. Lewis White Beck. Indianapolis: The Bobbs-Merrill Company, Inc., 1969

Kierkegaard, Søren. *Fear and Trembling* [1843], trans. Walter Lowrie. New York: Doubleday, 1954

Marx, Karl and Friedrich Engels. *The Communist Manifesto* [1848]. London and New York: Verso Books, 1998

St. John of the Cross. *Ascent to Mount Carmel* [1578–88], in *The Complete Works of Saint John of the Cross*, trans. and ed. by E. Allison Peers. Wheathampstead, Hertfordshire: Anthony Clarke, 1935

Sartre, Jean-Paul. *Being and Nothingness – A Phenomenological Essay on Ontology* [1943], trans. Hazel E. Barnes. New York: Pocket Books, 1956

Schiller, Friedrich. *On the Aesthetic Education of Man – in a Series of Letters* [1795], trans. Elizabeth M. Wilkinson and L. A. Willoughby. New York: Oxford University Press, 1967

Schopenhauer, Arthur. *The World as Will and Representation*, Volume I [1819], trans. E. F. J. Payne. New York: Dover Publications, Inc., 1969

Shirer, William. *The Rise and Fall of the Third Reich – A History of Nazi Germany*. New York: Fawcett Crest, 1950

Tanahashi, Kazuaki, ed. *Moon in a Dewdrop — Writings of Zen Master Dogen*. New York: North Point Press, 1985

Wittgenstein, Ludwig. *Philosophical Investigations*, trans. G. E. M. Anscombe. New York: Macmillan Publishing Co., Inc., 1953

Index